1 $\underline{^{25}}$

D1263949

THE
HUMAN
QUEST

THE HUMAN QUEST

A SEARCH FOR MEANING THROUGH LIFE AND DEATH

Virgil Elizondo

Our Sunday Visitor, Inc.
Huntington, Indiana 46750

Nihil Obstat:
Rev. John Reilly, S.J.
Censor Librorum

Imprimatur:
✠Patrick F. Flores, D.D.
Auxiliary Bishop of San Antonio
December 12, 1977

©Copyright Our Sunday Visitor, Inc. 1978
All rights reserved. No part of this book may be reproduced or copied in
any form or by any means — graphic, electronic, or mechanical, including
photocopying, recording, taping, or information and retrieval systems —
without written permission of the publisher.

ISBN: 0-87973-735-2
Library of Congress Catalog Card Number: 77-95164

Cover Design by James E. McIlrath

Published, printed and bound in the U.S.A. by
Our Sunday Visitor, Inc.
Noll Plaza
Huntington, Indiana 46750

735

*Dedicated to
my parents and sister
with whom I have discovered
the true meaning of life.*

contents

Origins of Evil
Description of Sin

Part Two: The Weakness and Foolishness of God

Part Three: The Divine-Human Adventure

Appendices

introduction

The first edition of this book was an effort to synthesize some of the new and enriching ideas of contemporary theology, scripture, liturgy, and the behavioral sciences. It was directed to the "grass-roots" catechist. This new, revised edition is motivated by the same purpose and is addressed to the same group of listeners: those whose charism of teaching for the community urges them to proclaim the Christian message in an ever-renewed, ever-renewing way. Much is updated in this revised study, but the inspiration for it remains the same as that of the original work: the words of Father José Calle, S.J., who brought out in a profoundly simple way how the basic yearnings and aspirations of man are the first whisperings of God's revelation to man. It is upon these basic yearnings and aspirations that subsequent revelation builds.

Catechesis, according to the "Pastoral Constitution of the Church in the Modern World," must begin with man. It must seek to reveal man to man. "The truth is that only in the mystery of the incarnate Word does the mystery of man take on light." "Christ, the final Adam, by the revelation of the mystery of the Father and his love, fully reveals man to man himself and makes his supreme calling clear." (GS-22) "Thus, in language intelligible to each generation, she (the church) can respond to the perennial questions which men ask about this present life and the life to come, and about the relationship of one to the other. We must therefore recognize and understand the world in which we live, its expectations, its longings, and its often dramatic characteristics." (GS-4)

For each new generation, the Good News must be proclaimed in ever new ways that correspond to the existential forms and ways of knowing of contemporary man. Catechetical change has to be brought about through specialized groups. With this in view, it is essential that pastors, theologians, catechists, psychologists, and sociologists enter into serious dialogue and work together in order to know the needs of each new generation, and discover new ways of expressing the Living Word. As the delegates to the 1977 International Synod of Bishops said in their important "Message to the People of God": "The yearnings of the young for creativity, justice, freedom and truth must be the starting point of all educational activity." (*Origins: NC Documentary Service,* November 10, 1977, p. 323)

The Documents of Vatican II and the Medellin Papers are a primary source for these adult catechetical themes. The ideas of Karl Rahner, Hans Küng, Teilhard de Chardin, Paul Tillich, Piet Schoonenberg, Hans Urs von Balthazar, Rudolf Schnackenburg, and the emerging thought of Latin America and of Third World theologians can be found in these pages, along with ideas of the staff of the East Asian Pastoral Institute. They all influence the present reflections on the human tensions: life-death, freedom-slavery, responsibility-escapism, community-egoism, and collective solidarity-ghettoism. I have endeavored to present the ideas, not as clear-cut blocks that together make up a building, but more as the gradual strokes of the artist that often overlap but eventually blend together to present a beautiful and meaningful picture. I am convinced that the Christian Message is far too rich in content and in meaning to be captured by words alone.

As a former student of chemistry, biology, and mathematics, I share the fascination for the physical sciences, a fascination that I have discovered in people today. I truly believe that, while not "providing God," the sciences manifest more and more both the evident and the hidden glories of our evolving world.

While everyone agrees that the world is evolving, not all agree on the direction that this evolution is taking or where it is ultimately leading us. I personally believe that the direction of this evolution cannot be explained except in and through Christ; also, I believe that it is in the context of an evolving universe that the meaning of Christ can be more fully appreciated by men today.

The primary purpose of this work is to develop a catechesis for 20th century adult Christians seeking to deepen their understanding and appreciation of their faith. The ideas presented in this work are not original, but attempt to synthesize in a simple way the ideas of the great thinkers of today's world. It seeks to explain the basic Christian notions of Creation, the Purpose of Life, Sin, the Incarnation and Redemption, the Church, the New Life of Christians, the Human Mysteries of Suffering, Death, and Life Everlasting. The approach is more descriptive than definitive. It is personalistic, existential, phenomenological, scientific, scriptural, and most of all, I hope, meaningful for the audience for whom it was prepared — the average priest and adult.

part one

The Strength
and Wisdom
of Humanity

chapter one

Critical Questioning

Preliminary Thoughts

From our earliest years, we begin to ask questions. As we grow, we seek to know the meaning of the realities that we encounter around us; increasingly, our questions become more penetrating. We begin to discover our uniqueness. We become aware that we are conscious, and begin to ask the meaning of this consciousness. Who am I? What is life? Why am I here?

These questions are asked by every person, yet each one seeks the answers in different ways. The man who is sitting in his comfortable den enjoying a drink after a successful day will view life differently than the man who is facing the end of another day without money to buy the necessary drugs for his sick child. The "problem of life" is one thing for the university student discussing it over a few beers. It is something else for the man coming home from another long, tiresome, uneventful day of work at the factory. Life will be seen quite differently by the sincere social worker who is truly interested in people, and the loan shark who is only interested in people's money. Yet all, in one way or another, seek the meaning of life.

As humanity evolves, man discovers more and more that vast complexity called Man. We continue to discover the meaning and working of creation, to learn how to improve and manipulate nature, to master the universe, yet the basic questions are still asked by every person at every stage of history. The more we discover about our universe, the more we seek to know just who is man? Who is woman? Who am I?

From a simple analysis of experience, from the discoveries of our education, and from the demands of daily living, we begin to discover that there is a lot more to life than mere existence. Science unfolds to us the gradual and beautiful evolution of the cosmic order toward a greater complexity and perfection. Man is conscious that, here and now, he is a real part of the evolving world in which he lives. We gradually experience the various modalities (aspects or dimensions) of our existence — joy, sorrow, pleasure, pain, fulfillment, frustration, success, failure. We are aware that life moves on. We cannot slow it down; we cannot undo the past. We can, to some extent, condition the future, yet this conditioning is always contingent on many factors, known and unknown, controllable and uncontrollable. Is there any meaning to the paradox of life? Is there any purpose to life? Is true and lasting fulfillment possible? Are we free to shape our future, or are we simply slaves of blind forces?

Throughout time, man has sought an answer to the riddle of his existence. We begin our journey of discovery into the meaning of our existence and of the world around us when we come to the realization that people are finite. Life is not forever. People die, they are buried, and they are gone. It is quite a shock when we experience for the first time that someone we love has come to a definite end, whether it is only our pet puppy, or our mother or someone else we dearly love. The first confrontation with death is a major moment in our lives.

As our journey of discovery continues, we gradually come to the awareness of our own personal finiteness; some day, no one knows when or how, I too will die. I am uncomfortable in the knowledge of my own finiteness, yet this uneasiness can open the door to the infinite, to the reality beyond self that is the key to the riddle of life. How does man answer, or seek to answer, the all-important question of his existence?

Reflections of the Average Person

Some people do not want to face reality. They accept the things they like, but run away from things that displease them. When they see danger, their immediate impulse is to run away. They do not even want to know themselves, to look into their inner selves, for fear of what they might discover. It is more common today for people to run away from themselves than to encounter themselves. It is much easier to seek to know another than to seek to know oneself. Self-knowledge can be painful. Why? Implicitly, there seems to be within us something that makes us want to be infinite and perfect. Yet we are aware of our limitations, failings, and finiteness, and the conscious knowledge of this can be bitter and quite painful. It is difficult to admit personal deficiencies or limitations. In many ways, our modern society is one of evasion, of running away from reality. Should we face ourselves honestly, or is it better to evade reality?

Some try to block out knowledge of the ugliness and problems of society, as such knowledge can cause pain or anguish and evoke a sense of personal responsibility. They want laws to eliminate beggars from the streets, to keep the poor in ghettos and out of sight, to put the elderly and the incurable into rest homes, to hide what is not beautiful or useful. Streets, parks, and homes should be beautiful and well-kept to give the impression that everything is fine. They call for all-out efforts to hide what should not be, but not for money or energy to change things to what they should be. Urban renewal, for example, has come to be known among the poor as urban removal. The poor are pitched out of the downtown area, relocated in the sticks, and forgotten.

Many people today fear physical discomfort and think that modern medicine can cure everything. Chesterton wrote that man does not love his body; he fears it. It seems that consciousness of bodily discomfort reminds us of our physical limitations, and eventually of death. In spite of miracle drugs and remarkable operations, people still die. We have not succeeded in eliminating death, yet we try to forget it and act as if it were not a reality.

The quest for eternal youth and undiminishing physical beauty has become a part of contemporary America. When a woman begins to grow old, cosmetics, health spas, and plastic surgery can be called upon to restore the fresh, young, and innocent look of eighteen. Men are encouraged through advertising to look like the Marlboro-man. Unfortunately, we tend to fantasize about our youth and dwell exclusively on our physical desirability, while forgetting the insecurities we experienced as youths. It is an immature attitude common in our society. Life is seen as a here-and-now happening without consideration for future consequences. Old age is regarded as a defect of nature. In more sophisticated and scientific ways we are still seeking the fountain of youth of Ponce de León. Should our old people be relegated to special apartments and complexes for senior citizens and be kept isolated from others? Do we view life as a beautiful process of growth and becoming, or is old age to be feared?

For some people life appears to be a mere game, and serious matters are to be overlooked. They join the happy-go-lucky crowd, go to parties, enjoy themselves, but never discuss religion, politics, or anything of grave importance. They just have a good time.

Then there are those who hold few personal convictions but simply go along with whatever is fashionable. This is depersonalization to the utmost, for the person ceases to be, and only the multitude exists.

The more serious evaders of personal reality are those who seek to live assumed roles so intensely that they come to identify role as the totality of their lives. Take, for example, the business executive who sacrifices his home and children to his own ambition, the monsignor who is so concerned with his role as "monsignor" that he doesn't let his real person shine forth, the politician who follows the rule of expediency — anything is all right as long as it assures reelection. Perhaps unintentionally and unconsciously, they falsify reality in the worst possible way and end up betraying themselves. Getting the job done or accomplishing private goals becomes the obsession of the person, while human relationships fade into the background. Thus, living the role successfully is the goal, and success in the goal, in our contemporary mythology, is equated with happiness.

Success and happiness is signaled to the community by purchase of a new home in the suburbs, with all the anointed amenities: swimming pool, the shopping center close by, tennis courts, and even security guards for protection against intruders. Is this paradise, or prison? Is such a suburb a pleasant place to live, or the institutionalization of depersonalization in tastes, values, and styles?

Ivory-tower idealism is another form of subtle escape for those who do not want to contaminate themselves with the mud of the real world into which they were born and of which they are a part. They retreat into a theoretical and intellectual world of their own and have as little as possible to do with the world of everyday worries. While not participating directly in the tensions of the world, they are willing to offer their carefully thought-out solutions to what they perceive to be the problems. The tragedy is that — all too often — the real problems are not touched.

At difficult moments, each of us avoids facing a problem by daydreaming, or refusing to acknowledge that a problem exists, or that we are responsible for it if we do acknowledge its existence. Sometimes this can give necessary time to confront the problem and seek a solution. This is normal and perhaps healthy, but in the extreme, a dangerous form of escapism from real life. To live fully, we need to be aware of ourselves and of the world around us. We need to accept both the joys and the sufferings of life, and face life's experiences.

There exist such individuals who seem gifted with the ability to adapt to the needs of the situation, who are able to seriously confront reality. Yet, whatever the challenge, they retain their balance and sense of humor. They can be accepting and convivial even in confrontation with others. What is it that enables them to laugh and to cry, to work and to play, to dream and to face disappointment, to fail and to succeed, to be realistic and idealistic, and rise above it all to maintain a beautiful sense of equilibrium and tranquility?

22

The Riddle of the American Existence

Why is it that, in our country, so many good people are destroying their own lives and the lives of others? Why do so many people who sincerely try to have healthy human relationships find themselves fighting one another, distrusting each other, and going their own separate ways in bitterness? Why is it that so many people work hard to become a success, and be happy, only to discover that in their success they have found emptiness? It almost appears that the more successful one becomes, the emptier life becomes.

A young, happy, struggling marriage, when husband and wife lived in a small apartment and existed on peanut butter and crackers, often loses meaning in later years of suburban living, dry martinis, and golf. After the couple moves to the prestigious suburb, and acquires everything one could want, they find that not only are they not speaking to each other, but they can't stand the sight of each other anymore. Yet neither one of them is a bad person; in fact, each of them is a beautiful person trying to do good and make a good life. What happens? Is happiness possible, or is it an illusion that merely creates more suffering by putting a wider chasm between reality and our hopes and ideals?

Why is it that, the more people have, the less they seem to truly live? The rich and famous members of the international jet-set are constantly on the move from one part of the world to another, but do they experience the simple inner joy of family and friends gathered for a backyard barbeque?

Many times, after years of preparation and untiring effort, the religious will find their ministry empty. Why? Is it a crisis of vocation or a crisis of person?

Without denying the existence of injustice and imperfection in our society, in general America has been a nation of hardworking, responsible people who have toiled to obtain what they have. America has been a nation of generous people willing to assist others during disasters, ready to lend a helping hand, and willing to send people to work in the Peace Corps, to do missionary work, and contribute to volunteer projects. Nevertheless, we find great suffering in the midst of material wealth.

Is it possible that we have taken some goals that are good and beautiful in themselves — success, happiness, security — but have translated them into a brick, mortar, and plastic reality that has not brought about fulfillment? The American dream, if translated into dollars and cents, property ownership, job, and social status has not really secured the happiness that we supposed it would.

Is it possible that we have created a vintage American mythology? It is true that every human being wants to be happy. In fact, the desire for happiness seems to be one of the fundamental human characteristics, yet how do we obtain this happiness? Is it through prestige? power? possessions? success? The person who has convinced himself that money, power, prestige, knowledge, or any other finite thing is a total answer to his quest for happiness will gradually and painfully discover it is not the case. His life will seem to be more of an infernal existence than a reflection of paradise on earth.

Just as it is possible for individuals to create myths for themselves, it is also possible for the members of a group to convince themselves of the absolute truthfulness of one of their collective biases. Nazi Germany considered those of pure Teutonic blood a master race. We, too, in America have created

24

the myth, "America, love it or leave it," that indicates an absolutizing of the American system as it is, with no room for critical questioning. Without critical questioning, growth is not possible, and when growth does not take place, decay sets in. At one time, Rome also absolutized its system and rejected critical questioning. Where is the great Roman empire today?

In seeking to find an adequate response to the riddle of life, some people have turned to science for the answer to our problems. Psychology is thought by some to have the answers that will lead to the emancipation of people from any type of enslaving relationship, be it with parents, family, friends, society, or even religion. Through the wisdom of psychology, man can become free and obtain happiness. Others have turned to the science of politics, and have claimed that all that is needed is an effective form of government. Some will say, "Democracy as we know it is the only way of government," while others say, "Communism is the only answer to man's problems." Others turn to physical science and technology and assume that science and technology can answer all of man's questions and provide solutions to all of his problems.

The danger with myths is that they express a conditioned view of reality. What is true in a given circumstance is enthroned into Truth that is applicable to all circumstances. With time, the conditioning becomes encrusted, and myth is absolutized. The absolute finally becomes a new god.

While some try to find the answer to man's questions and problems totally within man's world, others will seek to find the answer outside the world. Can the answers to the problems of the world be found in religion? Can it provide an adequate response to the human question? Or is it just one of our more grandiose myths?

In the contemporary quest for meaning, many people have turned to transcendental meditation, and tragically, even to drugs. While these might bring a certain amount of temporary individual fulfillment, real or imagined, the world beyond the individual continues in its state of destructiveness and suffering. When the momentary effects of the experience have passed, the aftermath seems to be even worse than the human condition prior to the experience.

Many people face reality squarely, but, not knowing how to cope with it, they tend to lose hope. This feeling of hopelessness can be the beginning of the road to despair. If a person feels that life is an absurdity, that the world has no purpose, he will not be able to seek genuine fulfillment, in spite of his natural yearnings. He is acting in a void, and his existence becomes useless. Is authentic living possible or should man do as the ancient Greeks did and become fatalistic and dance to the tune of cosmic forces?

Some Expressions of Man's Consciousness

In his search for meaning, man devises various ways of understanding the meaning of his existence. Some see the world as meaningful by itself, while others view the world as something for which the total meaning can only be discovered by going beyond the frontiers of its own limitations. That describes the basic distinction between the atheist and the theist.

For the modern-day atheist, the nonexistence of God is not the conclusion of an argument, but rather the starting point of a way of life. The stress is not on the nonexistence of God, which according to the nonbeliever cannot be proved or disproved, but on the absolute responsibility of man. The athe-

26

ist sees belief in God as an escape from responsibility. He claims that belief in God makes things too easy. For him, the responsibility of man is the starting-point. Man has come of age; he no longer needs to hide in the idea of God. He alone is now responsible for his condition and the condition of the world.

Atheism today is not limited to the philosopher or the scientist. For millions of people around the world, it is the accepted way of life. They do not even go to the trouble of denying God; they simply live without thinking about Him. To many, the idea of God today is one of historical interest and indicates the beliefs of people at one stage in the evolution of man.

In the past it was held that knowledge was a way to God. It was often proved that the existence of an ordered universe demanded the existence of a supreme intelligence and power to bring it into existence. Can it be that in trying to prove the infinite from the finite, we tried to prove too much and therefore ended up proving nothing?

The rapidly increasing discoveries of science have provided us with fuller understanding of the evolution of man, but they have led many to think of the idea of God as old-fashioned. Humanity has now come of age; we no longer need God. Man today feels that by combining science and technology, he can unite himself with nature, collaborate in some way with its evolution, and thus transform natural history into human history. He seeks to take into his own hands his destiny and that of the world; he assumes responsibility for the world and for humanity. Man receives the natural world as gift, but he feels and knows himself to be the creator of the technical world.

In going through its first stages of expansion, science rejected the idea of God in the name of science. God was the creation of the superstitious thought of infantile humanity. It was a useful crutch, but now it was necessary to kill the idea of God so man could come to the fullness of life. God could not be proved by science, therefore He did not exist!

We must be grateful to early scientific thought for making it clear that God cannot be proved by science! What an insignificant God He would be if He could be discovered in this way. Yet where does science, without the question of God, lead us? Does science have a built-in quality that will lead it to be creative and not destructive in its potential? Can science penetrate the inner mystery of the identity and destiny of the human person?

Marxism has certainly challenged traditional religions. It has hurled the charge that religion enslaves people and keeps them from progressing; religion teaches man to accept what is, rather than challenging him to work for what ought to be. Hence, the only salvation for man lies in the negation of God. If man is to be truly man, God is an obstacle that must be brushed aside. God appears as an artifact that political and religious rulers used in the past to keep the masses of the people in unending adolescence.

Marx describes religion as the cry of the downtrodden, the heart of the world without a heart, the spirit of an age without a soul; it is the opium of the people. Because man cannot find fulfillment in this world, he compensates with the image of another world. For Engels, religion directs man to empty himself of his true self and transform the essence of his humanity into the phantom of an unknown god in a great beyond.

With such ideas, and the state of organized religion being what it was, we can see why these men had to kill the idea of God. Only then might man be born. According to Marxism, it is only through the denial of God that man is truly born and is able to become the master of his existence. Could it be that the faulty image of God and of men presented as Christianity made the times ripe for the influence of Marxism?

For Marx, freedom is to be oneself; to be free is to be independent of all that is not self. A man who lives by the grace of another is dependent; hence, not free. Religion for him exacted total dependence upon another (God). Religion destroys the freedom of man. Since freedom is fundamental to man's nature, the more religious a man is, the less a man he is, and vice versa.

Probably the most original element in Marx's thought is the idea that human truth is neither natural nor metaphysical, but political, mediated by history. Truth is dialectic. He makes the analogy that just as private property must be suppressed because it separates the bourgeois from the proletariat, so, too, God must be suppressed because He separates man from man. For Marx, the believer is one who thinks that God alone is necessary if man is to attain his end. Atheism denies this and confronts man only with man.

Within the capitalist system, as within religion, man becomes a slave of his works. Within capitalism the fetish of merchandise and gold holds sway. Within religion, it is the fetish of gods that holds sway. Man is alienated from himself because he is alienated from his world. Man must be restored to himself so that he may attain the full satisfaction of a direct relation with other men without the mediation of an illusory

God. Man becomes the master of nature by becoming purely, totally, and exclusively man.

Could it be that in seeking to be purely, totally, and exclusively man, man will turn in upon himself rather than go beyond himself, and stop the growth of humanity? Will man find complete happiness solely within his world?

The conduct of many good-willed people who have rejected formal religion, but who nevertheless are dedicated to the alleviation of human suffering should confront the average Christian with serious and pressing questions. For even though the world seems an absurdity, to some of these people man in his here-and-now existence is not an absurdity, but an individual of flesh and bone who is suffering and whose suffering needs to be attended to. The image the church-going Christian too often gives the world is that his invocation of God is an attempt to run away from man's real problems. The average humanist today would say, "Let us face reality openly and do something about it. Let us not waste our time with talk, because even if there is a God, we can know little or nothing about Him and we certainly cannot manipulate Him. Let us not escape by running to God, but let us get in there and do what needs to be done." It often appears that many modern-day atheists have a far stronger sense of responsibility toward their fellow human beings than the average church-going Christian.

It seems that in past times, Christians were so concerned about the other world that they lost sight of this world, and thereby allowed the world to become a hell on earth for the masses of the people. Could it be that the pendulum is now swinging to the opposite extreme? And in being overly concerned about this world, are we now becoming enslaved within the corrals of self-centeredness, group-centeredness, and world-centeredness? Will this keep humanity from reaching past itself to the existence beyond this existence?

The Christianity that most of the adult world was born into and that most of the children still see practiced is the Christianity of pre-Vatican II. That idea of Christianity emphasized personal forgiveness, living according to the rules of fast and abstinence, Sunday Mass attendance, and the Commandments. It was concerned with formulas and recitation of the main tenets of the Creed. Almost exclusively concerned about the hereafter, it stressed salvation of the soul for the life to come. The idea of the Kingdom being here and now, the love of neighbor, the concern for each other as the "way" leading to the fullness of life; these concepts were, for the most part, neglected and ignored. This is not to say we were not concerned with good deeds, but good deeds were limited to Thanksgiving baskets, clothing drives, and occasional visits to the sick, all performed without a real commitment to introduce new life-styles in which mutual concern would be the ordinary way of life.

The atheist says that man is not responsible for his being, but that he is responsible for his existence. We had nothing to do with our being born into the world. To a certain degree, the world has shaped us, but we are now to shape the world. Life must not be sought up there in the heavens, but here on earth. Man has no destiny except the destiny that he works out for himself. He lives in a here-and-now situation and should not seek an explanation, for there is none to be found. He works, he plays, he sleeps, he dies — for what? He doesn't know. Has the modern atheist found the answer to the riddle of man's existence?

Why then is there an emptiness in the lives of so many people today? Could this lack of purpose be at the basis of so many disturbed lives, of the increased need for drugs, whether it be for sleeping-pills or LSD? Could this lack of meaning in man's life be the root of today's restlessness among so many people?

chapter two

Genesis

Psychologists, sociologists, anthropologists, theologians, philosophers, poets, and the ordinary man on the street: all shed some light on the great story of me. How did I grow and develop to be the unique me that I am today? No one has the complete answer to the question of life. There is no more fascinating study in life, not even that of the space trips and man's walk on the moon, than the study of life, and especially the story of my life.

Each Man's Life

It is difficult for us to imagine that a few years ago we were only inches long, weighed a few pounds, and were entirely dependent on others. The food we have eaten, the sports we have played, the education we received, the friends we have made, our home life, our work — all of our experiences have helped to make us what we are today. Gradually we have grown to be the unique individuals we are. The process of life itself is an extraordinarily complicated and mysterious business. I may try to ignore it, but I cannot escape the natural quest, the inborn curiosity to know me.

Each of us had a similar beginning. Psychologically, the

beginning of each person varied, but physically, it was the same: a man and a woman coming together in the sexual bond and forming the new human being. The miracle and mystery of life begins when the seed and egg unite in one of the fallopian tubes of a woman. At this instant, as a very minute, microscopic structure, the new individual has already received many of the characteristics that will be uniquely his throughout life. The submicroscopic genes, the architects and builders contained in the first cells, immediately begin to work at the blueprint for that unique life. Human growth, from the instant of conception, is rigorously patterned and controlled.

Who guides this complicated process? The mysterious inner forces at work within each cell! How do they do it? Science is discovering more and more each day, but there is still a lot to be learned. Each discovery sheds new light, and makes us realize more and more the greatness of the beautiful mystery of life.

The fertilized egg takes three or four days to drift down the dark fallopian tube into its future home. By the time it arrives in the womb, it has grown to a spherical cluster of several dozen cells. It continues to divide, and burrows into the lining of the womb that has been especially prepared to form a nest for the new embryo. In the first eight weeks of existence, this new life form will increase in length about 240 times and in weight one million times. In eight weeks we see the marvelous evolution from a tiny fertilized egg into a miniature baby or fetus.

How does the baby form? Were all the parts and organs of the body there already in miniature? Did they simply grow and develop? Scientists know today that the multiplication of cells enlarges the organism, the movement of groups of cells helps to shape the organism, and the differentiation of cells alters the form and function of cells to prepare them for different duties. The genes and chromosomes within the cells play the role of planners and work-supervisors in the evolutionary process of each individual.

Multiplication of cells begins almost at the instant of conception and for the first few days it is the only observable process in operation. Cells are reproduced in geometric progression: one cell dividing into two, then two into four, four into eight, and so on. As the embryo grows, cell movement begins. The cells in the outer ring will form the placenta. Those clumped on the innerside are the beginnings of the fetus itself. These inside cells will rearrange to form a two-layered disc, and thus the rearrangement continues with the multiplication of cells.

Multiplication and rearrangement sets the stage for the third process of growth: differentiation. By the end of the second week, groups of cells have embarked on the different paths, and will eventually result in the specializations necessary for the formation of the mature organism. This process is difficult to understand since there is no other process, either natural or man-made, paralleling the invisible chemical changes within developing cells, that bring about vastly differing forms and functions. Yet without differentiation, a complex organism such as man could not exist.

Following the built-in blueprints and the genetically preset schedule of construction, a cell or group of cells releases substances that cause neighboring cells to begin a new course of development. This cellular interaction not only induces individual cells to differentiate, but also prompts groups of cells to arrange themselves into functioning organs. These cellular interactions are an essential part of orderly development and organization of the body. Without the proper organization of the nerves, muscles, bones, and blood, the body will not function. The various systems of the body do not function in isolation but are interdependent. They are individually unique systems with particular roles to play, but each system requires the proper working of the others. Proper organization is the key to proper development, and it is likewise the key to good health in later life. Each system must be ready at the right time and in the right place for the growing fetus to survive.

The evolutionary journey of life goes on rapidly. When the body is formed and ready, the physiological forces of the mother prepare her to give birth to the baby within her. Suddenly the comfortable, shock-free, air-conditioned, carefree living within the mother's womb comes to an end. A new life begins with the moment of birth, the first traumatic experience of the individual's life: a painful end for the sake of new beginning.

What a difference there is between the shaping of a new life and the formation of anything else. A cook devotes a lot of time, know-how and energy to the cooking of a good meal. Scientists and technicians put time, energy, and brain-power into the development of a new product: temperature has to be controlled, pressure has to be adjusted, the samples have to be purified, the chemicals have to be carefully regulated. What elaborate plans, organization of workers, and materials are needed for the erection of new buildings! Yet the development of new life goes on almost unnoticed. Life reproduces in a mystifyingly hidden and simple way. The silent forces of Nature produce and reproduce the most complex, fascinating being in existence: man!

Life Itself

The origin of life is a deep mystery that only God knows. It seems that we will never know exactly how the organic developed from the inorganic, how transition from the nonliving took place. Even if the process could be repeated in the laboratory, it would give us only a partial answer, since we would still be ignorant of the exact conditions at the time.

If we follow Teilhard de Chardin in his beautiful and stimulating intuition of the world, there appears to be in all things a sort of inner force that makes the more simple forms of life inexorably develop into more complex forms. There seems to be a certain consciousness within all matter. This is especially evident in living things.

With the first act of creation, all spiritual and physical matter came to be. It existed in a sort of embryonic state. Over millions of years, this inner force has been bringing about the development of the lesser forms into higher forms of existence. We could say that there is only one creative act of God that has been going on for billions of years, is going on now, and will continue to go on.[1]

THE BIRTH OF MATTER — The universe shows evidence of being in a process of becoming that has been going on for eons. According to one theory, billions of years ago an infinitely large number of similar elementary particles were distributed throughout space. We are told not how they got there, but that they were there. These basic particles became organized into atoms. The atoms, by the force they exerted on one another, were drawn together into huge aggregates of matter, stars.

By studying certain stars, some scientists have evolved

37

theories concerning the origin of our planet earth. The stars were hothouses where more complex atoms of matter might have been cultivated. In this way all the simple elements as we know them were developed. With the production of the elements, evolution of the stars had gone as far as possible, for the surfaces of the stars were too hot for the more complex molecules to form.

"Some thousands of millions of years ago," writes Fr. Teilhard de Chardin, "not, it would appear, by a regular process of astral evolution, but as the result of some unbelievable accident (a brush with another star? an internal upheaval?) a fragment of matter composed of particularly stable atoms was detached from the surface of the sun. Without breaking the bonds attaching it to the rest, and just at the right distance from the mother-star to receive moderate radiation, this fragment began to condense, to roll itself up, to take shape. Containing within its globe and orbit the future of man, another heavenly body — a planet this time — had been born."[2]

By its initial chemical composition, the early earth was the incredibly complex germ of everything that is earth today. From the beginning, the world carried prelife within itself.

THE BIRTH OF LIFE — After a long period of time, the earth's surface cooled off sufficiently to allow the formation of chains of molecules of the carbon type. These molecules were probably covered by a layer of water. Some of these carbon molecules gradually came together to form huge macromolecules that were to be the link between the molecules and the cell. The evolution of macromolecules was of incredible slowness.

The next envelope of our planet, the biosphere — the sphere of life — formed with increased and growing complexity.[3] Some of the macromolecules evolved to sufficient complexity and function to be almost alive. At some moment that would be difficult or even impossible to calculate, primitive life arose — the miracle of protoplasm and the living cell, at the same time so complex and so simple. It is still the stuff of the universe, only now "it has reached a higher rung of complexity . . . and advanced still further in *interiority*, i.e. in consciousness."[4] At this moment, life truly appeared upon earth.

The first living cells must have been infinitesimal when they originated from the macromolecules, maybe 1/5000 of a millimeter long. The formation of protoplasm was, many suppose, a singular point, an unparalleled moment in the process of evolution. If protoplasm was formed only once on earth, there is a deep organic likeness that stamps all living creatures, from bacteria to mankind.

This phenomenon is one of the principal landmarks in the evolution of the globe. It shows that the origin of living bodies is linked with a chemical transformation probably unprecedented and unrepeated in the history of the world. "Life was born and propagates itself on the earth as a solitary pulsation."[5] It is the propagation of that unique wave that we must now follow up to man and beyond man.

The phenomenon of the gradual evolution of life seems almost impossible to trace, yet there is a distinct thread running through it, a continual expansion and deepening of consciousness.[6] The very "within" of the living mass carries it onward toward an even greater consciousness. "The essence of the terrestrial phenomenon shifted in a decisive way to become concentrated in that seemingly negligible thickness, the biosphere. The axis of geogenesis is now extended in biogenesis, which in the end will express itself in psychogenesis."[7]

For millions of years life continued on its upward journey. Animal life reproduced and evolved forward; it became more complex as the organs became more specialized and differentiated. In the primates the brain and nervous system are highly developed. The primates are at the head of the upward and onward march towards greater consciousness. Then after thousands of years, on the horizon of the world, the most powerful brains ever made by nature burst forth into flames and thought was born.[8]

THE BIRTH OF THOUGHT — "Morphologically the leap [from beast to man] was extremely slight, yet it was the concomitant of an incredible commotion among the spheres of life — there lies the whole human paradox."[9] What happened between that last strata in which man was absent and the next, in which the geologist is dumbfounded to find the first chipped flints? What is the true measure of this leap?

"It is true," writes Teilhard de Chardin, "that in the end, from the organic point of view, the whole metamorphosis leading to man depends on the question of a better brain. But how was this cerebral perfectioning to be carried out . . . if there had not been a whole series of other conditions realised at just the same time? If the creature from which man issued had not been a biped, his hands would not have been free in time to release the jaws from their prehensile function, and the thick band of maxillary muscles which had imprisoned the cranium could not have been relaxed. It is thanks to his two-footedness freeing the hands that the brain was able to grow; and thanks to this, too, that the eyes, brought closer together on the diminished face, were able to converge and fix on what the hands held and brought before them — the very gesture which formed the external counterpoint of reflection. . . .

40

Surely the smallest thing formed in the world is always the result of the most formidable coincidence — a knot whose strands have been for all time converging from the four corners of space . . . the birth of intelligence corresponds to a turning in upon itself, not only of the nervous system, but of the whole being."[10] From the grain of matter, we proceed to the grain of life, and to the grain of thought.

Man was born. Yet just as the appearance of the first cell marked but the beginning of the new age of the biosphere, which was to grow and reproduce over the thousands of years to come, so the appearance of the first man marked but the beginning of a new era of the noosphere. It was just another era in the evolution of the world, but what an era was born! Man was born, with infinite capabilities of determining himself and his surroundings. A totally new being had come into existence, capable of reflection, of thought, of planned and calculated action.

This new being was quite unique on earth, but it would be up to him to put his powers into action. For the first time, there was a being capable of building up and tearing down, of thought, reflection, logic, and of intellectual laziness and irrational activity. He was capable of great virtues and deplorable vices, of dynamic love and of destructive hatred, of creative work, and of annihilating laziness. Man the undetermined would henceforth seek to guide and control the various dimensions of determined reality. How did man get along with his world? This is the story, replete with both beauty and tragedy, that we hope to develop in the following pages.

It is difficult to see how anyone who studies the beautiful and inspiring evolution of our world and of man himself cannot ask himself some basic questions about the origin and purpose of the world, of life and of man. The evolutionary process over billions of years has been leading to the formation of man, and now man has taken over.

Evolution today continues not only by the inner forces at work in all nature, but also through the extrinsic forces at work upon nature. The constant efforts of the scientist and technician to understand, control, improve, and guide the forces of nature are gigantic steps in the growth of man and his world. At the same time this drive to use the forces of nature is being used to bring about the massive destruction of man and his world. The more man discovers the workings of nature, the more power he has at his disposal. Power is either creative or destructive, depending on how it is used by man.

For our purpose, it is sufficient to stop at this point of the evolution of the world and of man. We will continue our scientific-theological discussion at a later point. In the beginning of our discussions, we stated that God began to reveal Himself to man from within the heart of man. Since man comes from the stuff of the world, we might go a step further and say that God has been continually revealing Himself through the marvels of His evolving creation.

BIRTH OF RELIGIOUS THOUGHT — Throughout the ages man has sought to discover how life started. He has used the science, philosophy, and language of his day to record beliefs in his origins. Man has done the best he could with the science and equipment of his day. Today we have scientific opinion to throw light upon our origins. Only in recent times have we had the tools to look closely into our ancient past. Man has always been, and will always be, interested in his origins because such knowledge augments his understanding of the meaning of life.

42

Myths of the Ancient Past — The farther back we go into history, the more we discover how hard man had to struggle to survive. Tribal wars were common. Food was not abundant and man had to till the land with sweat and effort to win a meager crop. "An eye for an eye and a tooth for a tooth" — every man was out for himself. Human life meant little. Crime, murder, robbery — the survival of the fittest was the rule. Human beings were objects to be used by whoever was powerful enough to control them. Women were for the pleasure of men. Yet always man was seeking answers. Who am I? Where did I come from?

In this world of war and brutish struggle for survival, it is not surprising that people should imagine the origins of the world to have taken place in war and struggle among divine beings. The ancient Babylonian myth, known as the Enuma Elish, pictures creation of the universe, earth, and man as the result of a fierce battle among the gods. Aspu and Tiamat, male and female deities, begot the gods. Apsu is slain by his offspring, Ea. Tiamat, after an epic battle, is slain by Marduk, Ea's son. From the remains of the carcass of Tiamat, Marduk fashions the world. Kingu, Tiamat's counselor, is slain and from his blood, mankind is fashioned.

In another part of the world, Egypt had its own creation myths. In one myth the god Atum-Re, after being produced from Nun (the waters of chaos), fertilized himself, then sputtered out Shu (air) and Tefnut (moisture) and transferred his vital force into them. They in turn produced Geb (earth), Nut (sky) and other gods. From the tears of the god Ra, man came into existence. At Memphis the god Ptah was revered as the creator and all living beings were believed to have come into existence from his heart, thought, and tongue.

43

We know much less about the ancient creation myths of Canaan. The god El in the Canaanite pantheon bore the title creator of the earth, and his consort Asherah, progenitress of the gods. Baal, their son, was the god of rain and storms. Sometimes Baal was considered as the greatest of the gods, superior to the older El.

In different ways man explained his origins. In most of these ancient myths, creation and life are attributed to some preexisting deity, to union between male and female deities, or to some sort of battle fought between the gods from which the world and man came forth.

Ancient Religions — Not only do the ancient myths shed light on man's constant quest for the origin and meaning of his life, but the ancient religions also give some interesting insights. It is clearly not within the scope of this work to give a comparative study of the religions of man, but we will look briefly at the main currents of religious thought that have developed from the living experiences of individuals and communities.

Hinduism — Sometime between 2000 B.C. and 1500 B.C. Hinduism began to appear in the subcontinent of India. It never claimed to have a founder, but advanced, in some measure, from the experience of suffering in the people of that area. People reflected and realized that the world was unconscious of their suffering and even of their existence.

They suffered, and yet there was beauty and tranquility in the world. There was beauty in the stars, in a flowing stream, in a glowing sunset. Plants grew and enjoyed tranquility in the midst of man's suffering. All around him man saw that there was beauty and harmony in nature, but not in himself.

People began to question the meaning of existence. They suffered, yet nature was beautiful and peaceful. They did not question how people or the universe was created, but assumed that the Universe *is*. The world was Brahman, the Limitless One . . . Incomprehensible is that Soul, unlimited, unborn, not to be reasoned about, unthinkable . . . He whose soul is space! . . . The world is thought by him, and in him it disappears . . . the whole world is Brahman.

For the Hindu, all creatures, all things, all peoples are ultimately part of the One. Contrary to our belief, there are no individual souls or persons, but we are all part of Brahman — the One. The true self of a man and the world are one. By transcending the world of the individual self, the human soul knows its complete identity with Brahman; it is entering Moksha (salvation). To dissolve oneself completely into the One is the only source of happiness.

How does one enter Moksha? By removing oneself from the world of Maya or illusion. This is the world of the senses. One must enter into oneself to know the absolute oneness of all being. The tree and I are one . . . the cow and I are one . . . all creation and I are one. . . . Happiness can only come through uncompromising and extreme asceticism. A complete deliverance from the world of suffering and misery is had through a conscious and disciplined identification with the One. Man does not seek to improve his lot or his world, but he seeks only to escape it. The seemingly real world in which he lives is only an illusion, and Brahman is the only real existing entity. To realize this is Moksha.

Buddhism: Around the year 500 B.C. Gautama, who became known as The Enlightened One or Buddha, discovered that deliverance could not come through either the extreme sensuality of the common man or through the extreme asceticism of Hinduism. The only way to deliverance from misery was the middle way. He had scrupulously tried to live in the way of the Brahman but had found it to be impossible. He tried hard and failed.

Failure led him to discover the middle way. In the middle way, he found himself to be without any desire; in fact, he discovered himself to be neither satisfied nor dissatisfied. In this state, he found peace. He had entered into an earthly foretaste of Nirvana. It is the knowledge of the middle path that avoids either pleasure or mortification and gives enlightenment that eventually leads to the heavenly peace of Nirvana.

To the Buddha it was useless to waste time speaking about the eternity or noneternity of the world. Philosophical speculation of any kind was out-of-place because it was useless. The central point of interest to the Buddha was why do men suffer, and the only real question for man is "what is the path leading to the cessation of suffering?"[11]

American Indian: The great Indian civilizations of Latin America reveal another aspect in the religious thought of the peoples of ancient times. The civilizations of the Incas of Peru, the Mayas of Central America, and the Aztecs of Mexico had their origins around the year 2500 B.C.

In the beginning, theirs was a simple life of hunting, fishing, and agriculture. As their civilization grew, tribal wars and the building of great cities began to take place. For the most part, these civilizations never went beyond the neolithic age. Their use of metals was mainly ornamental. Life was little more than the daily struggle of staying alive. A good life consisted of sufficient nourishment and the absence of sickness.

It is not surprising to see that the principal function of

the religions of these ancient peoples was to ensure life, health, and sustenance. Their prayers and rituals revolved around the deities who governed the various aspects of life.

Their ideas on the origins of the world were quite complex, a fusion of myth and local tradition. With each new conquest the myths grew, as the conquered people were obliged to take up the religion of their conquerors but did not have to give up their own. The god who created all things was not of too much importance, as he was believed to have passed on various assignments to the other deities. It was the lesser gods who really had control over individual and national destinies. The complexity of the Aztec cosmogony would rival the most elaborate of the Greek mythologies.

In contrast to the religions of India and Asia, the American Indians never considered the world to be an illusion or something from which to escape; they accepted life as a reality, and tried to live it in the best way they could, both physically and morally. Their religious beliefs led them to seek the intercession of the various deities who they believed controlled the forces of nature. To survive man had to keep the gods happy. Famine, sickness, or any misfortunes were a sign of the displeasure of the gods. To keep the gods happy, they offered sacrifices, the fruits of the land and animals. Only in later periods did human sacrifices take place.

The most recent of these civilizations, the Aztecs, put great emphasis on human sacrifices. One of the most important of the deities was Huitzilopochtli, the war-god and symbol of the sun. For life to continue, he had to be well nourished, vigorous, and healthy. Since his major source of sustenance was human blood, human sacrifices were necessary. To secure victims for him to feed on, religious wars were undertaken and the hearts of the conquered were offered to him as nourishment. Their bodies were then eaten by the people in the belief that through this rite, they entered into communion with the deity to whom the hearts had been offered.

The Hebrews: Alongside the great civilizations of the ancient past a small nation existed that was never famous for its culture, its art, its armies, its conquests, or its discoveries, yet the relatively unknown and insignificant Hebrew nation made the greatest contribution of all to man's constant quest for meaning and ultimate reality. The depth of their thought far surpassed all others of their times.

Though they had their beginnings sometime around 1900 B.C., they did not reach the high point of their reflections until the middle of the final century preceding the coming of Christ. As the Hebrews reflected on their history and celebrated in their liturgy the great events that gave birth to their nation, they came to know a supremely powerful and personal God who involved Himself in the affairs of man. Israel constantly experienced the power and the concern of Yahweh: in the deliverance from Egypt, during their forty year stay in the desert, by the victories in the Promised Land, in their everyday lives.

Yahweh used the elements of nature for the salvation of His people. The people not only experienced the power and generosity of Yahweh, but they learned of the true and hidden meaning of His works through the words of the Prophets. The prophets were always there to interpret the events to the people, for it was only through their words that reality became truly real.

God not only loved and protected His people; He was the source of all life. Without Him, there could be no purpose for existence. God gave life to each individual. Life was union with God through living God's laws. Death was separation from God. "I have set before you life and death, the blessing and the curse. Choose life, then, that you and your descendants may live. . . ." (Deuteronomy 30.19)

Through His deeds and words, God was constantly making Himself and His ways known to man and inviting man into friendship with Him. The Hebrews came to know their God as completely other (transcendent) — all-powerful, everywhere and all-knowing — yet completely immersed in the affairs of man (immanent), as close to each man as man is to himself. The God of the heavens was the intimate friend of man.

The Hebrew was the recipient of so many of God's blessings. When did all these blessings begin? With Moses? With the Covenant of Sinai? With Abraham, the father of the Hebrews? Since their God was the all-powerful and always present God of all nature, His blessings must have started even before Abraham. They gradually experienced Yahweh as the lord and master of all nature. He was not only their local God, he was also the God of nations. Against Him, all other gods were helpless.

The Hebrew sees his God not only as the Supreme Governor of the universe, but as the Creator. Creation is the first manifestation of God as the source of life and goodness. The biblical account of the creation was not intended to be an eyewitness report of what went on; neither was it intended to be a scientific study of the nature of creation. In speaking about creation, the Hebrews used the myths that were current at the time, but gave them a completely different meaning.

In contrast to the ancient myths, the biblical God of creation is pictured as the supreme, all-powerful One whose Word brings matter and life into existence. He fights no battle with other gods; there is no union of the gods to produce lesser gods or creatures. God simply speaks, and there *is*. Everything that God creates is good. There is no duality, no creation of good and evil. The Hebrew saw creation not so much an act but as a process. God is not so much the creator as He is the creating one.

The creation narratives date from the time of the Prophets (900 to 500 B.C.). They express the faith of Israel in looking back at its origins. This does not make these stories false. It is simply the preface of the book that is written when the book was complete, or nearly complete. Israel saw in creation a vivid manifestation of God as the source of Life. Israel had experienced the power and the love of her living God. It was not an abstract knowledge of God, but rather the knowledge that evolves from the intimate relationship of one person with another. These actions were expressed in a poetic and extraordinary way.

There was a gradual progression of God's entry into human history as we see it recorded in the Bible. In fact, the great accomplishment of Israel was to be mature enough to recognize that saving history did not begin with the Exodus or with Abraham, but with creation. The first saving event is in fact the beginning of history — the emergence of man.

The high point of God's creation is man who is made to the image and likeness of God. In the context of the creation narratives we see the true meaning of this statement. God is a creating God. Man made to the image of God is to be a creating man. The modern atheists are so right when they remind us that man has come of age. Man has to discover that to be

50

his full self, to be truly the image of God, he is not to be a passive creature. He must be an active, creating being who shares responsibility for the present condition of the world. To be fully persons we are to use our potential to develop the earth and to make it truly a garden of happiness for all. God has made all things for us. We must neither fear nor worship the powers of nature but learn to use them.

The narrative of the Bible is simple and beautiful. God brought the cosmos out of chaos. Out of the cosmos He fashioned man to His own image and gave him dominion over all the earth. It is now man's job to imitate the Creator by making full use of his creative abilities. Every discovery that will truly benefit man and his world is an imitation of the creative work of God. It is a living-out of the mission of humanity in which we use our talents to the fullest, bringing about the perfection of people and the world.

Here is indeed a remarkable contrast with the idea of man and his world in the ancient religions of Egypt, Babylon, India, Asia, and America. In creation there are no wars and struggles, but the simple all-powerful Word of God bringing life into existence. The world is not to be escaped, but rather to be used, enjoyed, and developed. The all-powerful God loves man and seeks his happiness.

Human sacrifices were never permitted in the Hebrew religion. It was the sacrifice of living according to the Divine Will that God asked, and the Divine Will was precisely the way to man's true happiness. God truly comes to man in a visible and audible way so that man may find the way to God. It is only gradually that man, through God's constant revelation, will discover the full meaning of life and find the way to the fullness of life.

chapter three

Humanity:
A Mistake of the Gods?

Personal Experience

It does not take a very perceptive or well-informed person to know that we live in a troubled world. Our current history includes world wars, cold wars, an increased suicide rate, countless murders, rape, blackmail, enforced economic slavery, the popularization of the playboy philosophy, nervous breakdowns, wild demonstrations and their brutal repression. The litany could go on.

Violence and crime are not only daily news items; they are also glorified in movies, television programs, novels, and even in children's toys. With only a flick of the magic wand of mass media, human savagery of every sort enters the living room to become family entertainment. The experts tell us movies and television programs are not formative of morals and culture, but rather projections of the current culture and moral trends in society. This glorification of wickedness and brutality reveals the angry world in which we live and of which we are a part.

Misconduct, crime, and violence are a very real part of each man's life. Even an analysis of our own personal life will show us that we live in a troubled world. In our own simple, personal, non-newsmaking way, we are contributing to this ever-growing evil in the world. We are personally responsible for the fact that the evolution of the world is not progressing as rapidly as it could.

Many would be ready to say nonsense at this point. They would be quick to point out that the world moves on with or without us. One individual makes very little difference in the evolution of the world. Even louder would be the objection that we have personally contributed to the growing evil in the world. Most ordinary good people are conscious that they have not killed anyone, stolen, or ruined anyone's reputation. They are usually polite and easy to get along with. The average person would say emphatically, "I haven't done anything wrong."

For many people it is really not so much a question of doing something wrong, but rather not doing anything about a situation that is wrong. Millions of people hear the evening news with its usual crimes of the day, spend a few minutes complaining about the ineffective police who are good only for issuing speeding tickets, and then peacefully go off to bed, satisfied with themselves because they have done a good day's work. People know there are thousands of hungry, uneducated, unskilled, unloved, unemployed people who are barely existing on the "other side" of the city. They excuse themselves from doing anything by dismissing the poor as "those lazy bums who cannot be helped. . . . They are happy, why disturb them?"

Others are quick to complain about the government, the school, the church, or even the club. They are either doing too much or not doing enough. Ask the ones who complain the loudest to get themselves involved, and their response comes fast, "It's their job; that's what they get paid for. Besides, I'm too busy." It is sad that so many seem to follow the philosophy: complain about what others are trying to do, but don't try to do anything yourself. You may get criticized.

Examining my own personal experience, I could ask myself: am I one of those who lives day after day, surrounded by the people with whom I live and work, without ever showing any real concern for their personal needs, anxieties, and emptiness? Do I treat them as objects, not really seeing them as warm, living persons who are full of feelings, emotions, passions, and ideas? Sometimes the most dedicated persons fail on this count. They become so involved in their work that they fail to treat their co-workers as human beings.

Take, for example, a very dedicated teacher who spends long, difficult hours preparing lessons and evaluating the students' work. Such a teacher often becomes so wrapped up in seeing that the students learn the subject well that he never allows himself the joy of knowing his students as human beings. He will suffer great frustration and cause much suffering to the students because he thinks he knows his students. In reality he does not. He may know their intellects, but they are not just intellects. They are human persons who can only know and be known as persons. For such a teacher, the students are not persons but mere subjects of learning.

There are many good-willed ministers of God who are concerned with buildings, liturgical renewal, and the parish plant, yet they rarely have time to visit and know their parishioners personally. This type of person who loses himself in his work makes a contribution to the development of society in one way, but in another way he contributes to the growth and development of evil.

54

On the level of personal life, evil is the lack or limitation of love. Love is the psycho-moral energy that physically builds up the universe, the very bloodstream of human evolution. It alone can unite men and bring them to their final perfection. There is no other force capable of uniting people without destroying their personal identity. In fact, the greater the love, the greater the degree of acceptance of another as unique self.

True love will say to the beloved, "I love you because you are you." Egotistical love will say to the beloved, "I love you only because you are what I would like you to be." True love will not cease in times of crisis or difficulties, while egotistical love will cease with the slightest upset.

No doubt this is an oversimplification, but these two basic attitudes are at the base of virtue and vice. Consider the parable of the Good Samaritan (Luke 10.25-37). Place yourself in the position of the victim and you begin to appreciate what true love is. When you are in grave need, you do not make qualifications of the one who comes to help you.

Love is the key to the moral order and even the physical order. It is the only energy that is truly capable of furthering human progress. When one refuses to love, he is not only injuring his own person, but humanity as a whole. To the degree that I love, I am a person of virtue; to the degree that I limit my love or refuse to love, I am a person of vice. Virtue or vice cannot be legislated by any governing body, no matter how powerful. They have their source in the life of society and ultimately in the life of each individual.

The existence of evil and its destructive influence in our world is not something to be proved from psychology, philosophy, theology, or any other branch of science. It is an existential phenomenon, a datum of personal and collective experience that imposes itself upon me, whether I like it or not. If I want to eliminate it, I must seek to discover its source both in society and in the individual who makes up society.

Origins of Evil

In the physical world we are aware that there can be no summits without abysses. So it is with the history of the world. Within the evolutionary process, we seem to discover a certain mysterious "within" that guides all things towards greater complexity and perfection. Obstacles are overcome and the development of the cosmos proceeds on its path towards maturity.

Man gradually develops the vast powers of his mind, powers of analysis, discovery, synthesis, creative ability, and memory. Yet from the very beginning, man used his powers to free himself from dependence on his creator and from his responsibility to the world and his fellowman. He attempted to be sufficient unto himself. In trying to make himself "like gods" (Genesis 3.5), he fell away from God. Man created his own abysses of evil around his great summits of accomplishment.

As it continues along its mysterious paths, evolution is now capable of being guided by its new master, humanity. Yet because we are by nature free agents, we will not necessarily direct ourselves towards fulfillment. The beginning of human thought and reflection was a marvelous step forward in the evolution of the world. But thought in itself is a neutral force; man can use the powers of his mind to create or to destroy. Man as a thinking subject was moving forward; man as a developing person was a different story.

Through the sweep of the Bible, the development of

human evil appears in all its dimensions. The history of salvation is the tirelessly repeated attempt of God to draw man away from self-destructive and community-destructive activity. Man's evil activity gradually received the generic name of sin.

Several hundred years before the coming of Christ, especially during the time of the Prophets, the Israelites sought an explanation for the evil that they experienced in themselves and all around them. Their experience of God had always been of a saving and merciful God. God could not be the source of evil, yet evil existed. It had to have a beginning. How did it all begin?

In the ancient view of sacred history, the characteristics of a tribe or people were considered to have originated with the ancestor of the group. The Israelites knew that the evils afflicting them were common to all mankind: tribal wars, laziness, subhuman treatment of men, man's constant quest to be the supreme norm and judge of his own actions, disregard for human rights. If all this evil activity is characteristic of humanity, it must have been characteristic of the ancestors. It must have started with the first man and woman who brought this evil on themselves through their own fault. After this first fault, every man could apply to himself the words of the Psalmist: "Behold, I was brought forth in iniquity, and in sin did my mother conceive me." (Psalm 51.5)

The biblical description of man's sinfulness begins with the third chapter of Genesis. Therein we find a picturesque theology and psychology of temptation and sin. The dialogue between Eve and the serpent becomes more and more pointed. It ends with the serpent's outright denial of God's veracity and the insinuation that God is jealous of man. God had written within man's heart a way of life, but from the beginning

57

man allowed lesser creatures to tempt him and dictate to him.

Man is pictured as seeking independence from God and from his fellowman. He wanted moral autonomy and independence; he wanted to be a god unto himself so that he alone would be the norm of good and evil. It is easy to see from our own personal experience that such fruit is "... good for food, pleasing to the eyes." (Genesis 3.6) The desire for freedom without responsibility is as alluring as it is deceptive.

"And you will be like gods." Yes, man would become like the gods of the pagan world who could sit on their thrones and laugh and play while the world was suffering. The gods who watched the world were never concerned about its condition and never did anything to help. This was the pagan concept of the gods, and this was the temptation: to stay on the sidelines, uninvolved in the development of the world.

The preface of the Bible (Genesis 1 and 2) states that sin was committed and originating sin had begun. In these accounts of Genesis (Chapters 3-11), the devastating and destructive nature of sin is clearly brought out. Sin grows and increases like the small spark that lights the forest fire, or the small particle that begins the snowball that eventually becomes an avalanche. Adam is pictured as disobeying, Cain kills his brother, and the climax of evil is pictured in the Tower of Babel, where collective humanity conspires to be a god unto itself and make its own way to heaven. The epitome of evil has been reached; society has now rejected God's way in favor of its own.

The predicament began with Adam, and we inherited it. But we cannot blame it all on Adam, for humanity has been contributing to it throughout the ages. Each person within each generation has contributed his own personal and originating revolt by resisting or rejecting his share in the development of the world. In this way, the personal and collective sins of man ceaselessly proclaim and ratify the first disobedience at the dawn of the human race.

Original sin is pictured as the primitive transgression of primitive man, who nevertheless was sufficiently aware to reject God's invitation to become fully human and co-responsible for the development of the world. Descendants of Adam not only inherit this sin; they personally ratify it by adding to it their own personal sin. This is all the more serious because of their superior level of culture, more mature awareness of themselves, and a more complete mastery over the world in which they live.

Description of Destructiveness

Let us try to penetrate deeper into the nature of sin. The first chapters of Genesis bring out clearly how man refused to live up to the full stature of his manhood by abdicating his crucial place in the scheme of things. This abdication of his place as the lord of creation is what the Bible calls sin.

We have in the past seen pride as the basic element of man's sin. This is correct, provided we understand its meaning as the quest of man to become more while in reality becoming less. Seeking to become a god, in reality he becomes a creature not only unlike God but even less than human. "You will be like gods who know what is good and what is bad." (Genesis 3.5) It is so tempting to substitute oneself for God, to decide alone what is good and what is evil, to take oneself alone as the measure of all human conduct.[1]

The degrading element, which is brought out in the Genesis account of sin, is that man sold his birthright. He sold himself to the serpent (symbol of the world) by allowing it to control him rather than exercising control over the serpent. Man is pictured as allowing one of the animals to tell him what to do. There is a profound meaning behind this simple picture; man is pictured as surrendering his position of privilege and responsibility. Man has been made to master the world, but he has allowed the world to master him. From this moment there is trouble. The Bible pictures Adam as the man who at first will not be man, and then through his sin cannot be man. In the Bible Adam represents all men.

One of the best English words for bringing out the biblical notion of sin is sloth. Sloth is sitting back and allowing the winds and tides to sweep the ship along its path. It is a refusal to get out of the comfort of the playroom and into the arena of the world. It is the damning and self-destructing attitude of noninvolvement.[2]

Man can and should be proud that he is made to the image and likeness of the creating God and that he is invited by God to share responsibility for the development of the world. Man develops a false pride in himself when he allows himself to be controlled by the world, by the subhuman creature-gods (Genesis 3.1-7). This false pride in himself is sloth, and he becomes less than man. This is his determined or lackadaisical refusal to live up to his essential humanity.

The constant theme of the preaching of the Prophets, which is so timely today in our secularistic society, is that the man who attempts to build by himself will bring about his own ruin. Without God, man will advance at the expense of other men, principally of the small, the ignorant, the weak, and the helpless.

The Bible presents sin in its relationship to each man's

experience of his own personal sin. It does not prove the existence of sin, but simply states that sin exists in the world. Original sin is seen against the larger background of man's consciousness of individual and collective responsibility. The fall of Adam is considered less an isolated and static event than a power that grows with the growth of humanity itself.

part two

The Weakness
and Foolishness
of God

chapter four

Preparation of a New Creation

The Birth of Man: Evolution and Saving History

For millions of years, the world had quietly been evolving along its path towards greater complexity. The first phylum of life was born when the first living cell came forth from the right combination of molecules. The birth of life was a new plateau in the evolution of the world. During the millions of years that followed, new phyla of animals, ever more complex, gradually appeared from previous ones. Then, with no one to observe and record the facts, a new phylum broke through to the surface. Life became conscious of itself; thought was born; man was born. Man became capable of determining himself and his surroundings, capable of reflection, of logic, of art, of love, and of hate. Until then, life had been controlled by the universe. Henceforth man would control the universe and, consequently, life itself.

As we have briefly discussed in a previous chapter, the birth of man released a new force for future development. Man gradually became aware of his vast powers, but as the record of humanity indicates, he did not use these powers for the development of the human family but for his own personal gain. Current history is not basically different from the history of any age. Look at the tremendous amount of money, manpower, and effort that goes into the production of war equipment — into the support and training of armed forces with more powerful weapons to destroy and kill. We may be quick to respond that this is necessary. But hasn't humanity made it necessary?

The movie "2001: A Space Odyssey" shows the birth of thought. A primate discovers the use of a bone as a lever and immediately uses it to fight other primates. Hasn't this been the case for all of recorded history? We discover a new power and immediately we seek to use it for our own benefit, even if this means killing the man next door. Is not the history of humanity one of family fights, tribal wars, revolutions, civil wars, and world wars?

When thought was born, man was born, and with him came the power to love. Yet the records show that this power to love has, for the most part, lain dormant. Man has sought progress but progress through brute power, intrigue, killings, and war. The powerful have become more powerful at the expense of the poor, the defenseless, and the ignorant. Man has seen his fellowmen simply as commodities, as objects to be used and then discarded when they become useless.

The noosphere was born and man had developed as far as he could on his own. He had turned into himself so much that his self-love had made it impossible for him to reach further. Humanity was unable to go beyond itself. Thought in itself was not sufficient to energize man's development to the next stage. Humanity was in chaos. Would man, the crowning glory of the world, use his powers to destroy himself and his world?

Beginning of Saving History

Yet within struggling humanity a new force was quietly at work. God was gradually preparing the ground for a breakthrough. The decisive step was taken to remedy the situation; God entered the arena of human events.

"In carefully planning and preparing the salvation of the whole human race, the God of supreme love, by a special dispensation, chose for Himself a people to whom He might entrust His promises. First He entered into a covenant with Abraham (Genesis 15.18) and, through Moses, with the people of Israel (Exodus 24.8). To this people which He had acquired for Himself, He so manifested Himself through words and deeds as the one true and living God that Israel came to know by experienc[ing] the ways of God with men, and with God Himself speaking to them through the mouth of the prophets, Israel daily gained a deeper and clearer understanding of His way. . . ."[1]

This magnificent drama of God's activity with man began only about two thousand years before Christ. In His own gentle, mysterious way, God looked on mankind and chose an unknown, insignificant Bedouin named Abram to begin the greatest love story ever recorded. Why did God pick Abraham? He certainly was not powerful, rich, or especially desirable, yet God chose him as he was. God chose this semi-nomad from all the peoples in the world and made to him the promise of land and progeny (Genesis 13.14ff). God's pure, disinterested love for man began to shine forth.

Does this mean that before God's call to Abraham the world had been going along on its own while God had remained uninvolved? God has always been involved. What marks the beginning of God's saving activity through Abraham is not that God entered history for the first time, but rather that Abraham responded to God's call. God revealing and man responding marks the beginning of salvation history. Man became conscious of God's loving activity in his life, recognized the challenge of God's call, and responded to his challenge. That was the beginning of historical revelation.

Israel: The Growing Child

The human drama of the rearing of a child by a loving parent will help us to understand the drama of God's love for humanity. The parent must love, protect, and be patient. He must correct, rebuke, and punish when necessary, but he must, at the same time, not be overprotective and prevent healthy and normal growth. The parent's love must possess balance to stimulate proper growth of the child: to love but not to spoil, to punish but not repress, to protect but not enslave.

God the all-knowing, all-loving, perfect Father stepped into the history of man to bring forth a new life which humanity had not been able to achieve on its own. God called, Abraham answered, and a new child was born. The development of this child would take hundreds of years. After living for many years in a foreign land the descendants of Abraham were enslaved by the Egyptian Pharaoh (Exodus 1.7). Yahweh freed them from Pharaoh, guided them to safety through the Red Sea, nourished and fed them in the desert, entered into a covenant relationship with them at Sinai, and finally led them into the Promised Land. A group of uneducated, jealous, and complaining individuals had experienced the powerful, redemptive love of Yahweh (Exodus 20.2).

As a young child needs not only love but also instruction

and correction, so it was with Israel. God had delivered them from their bondage. From a motley group of people a new nation emerged. This new nation had to be forged; accordingly, the Supreme Psychologist of growth gave to Israel the Law (cf. Deuteronomy 4.5-8; 6.4-9).

No mature parent would bring up a child by telling him, "Love!" Rather he teaches the child to love and to be loved through explicit actions. Say "hello." Be polite to your uncle. Let your sister use your water colors. These actions are living examples of the command, "love not only yourself but others."

Israel recognized that the Law that Yahweh had given at Sinai was the Sign that they were God's own special possession and the object of God's special love. Israel often failed in the observance of the Law. In fact, the Old Testament might be said to be the record of Israel's unfaithfulness and God's constant faithfulness to the Covenant. It is the story of the world's greatest lover. After creating the world and being rejected by it, He still chose to re-create without destroying.

"My father was a wandering Aramean who went down to Egypt with a small household and lived there as an alien. But there he became a nation great, strong and numerous. When the Egyptians maltreated and oppressed us, imposing hard labor upon us, we cried to the Lord, the God of our fathers, and he heard our cry and saw our affliction, our toil and our oppression. He brought us out of Egypt with his strong hand and outstretched arm, with terrifying power, with signs and wonders; and bringing us into this country he gave us this land flowing with milk and honey." (Deuteronomy 26.5-9)

This was one of the early creeds of the Israelites; they believed because they had experienced the saving power of

God. They trusted in Yahweh, but not so much that they would completely change their way of life. People are living organisms, and as such they do not change easily or quickly. We know from modern psychology that change in the individual is very slow. From history we know that the change in nations is many times slower.

The Experience of Yahweh

While they were struggling through the desert and fighting for the Promised Land, the Israelites were very conscious of the presence and will of Yahweh. They realized that alone they were untrained, inexperienced, and powerless. Yet once they were established in the Promised Land and became powerful, they quickly forgot the real source of their power. The Chosen People continued to worship Yahweh, but their worship became formalism and empty ritual. It was in no way expressive of their daily living.

Israel had become the young adolescent struggling for liberation and total independence. Israel became like the youth who, against all good advice, drops out of school to conquer the world. He goes off, as did the rich young man in Luke (15.11ff.), to a far off land to make a fortune and name for himself. He is young, intelligent, bold, brave, and strong. He can stand alone. He needs no one to help him.

The people of Israel knew the way of Yahweh, but now that the young nation was coming of age, the other way, the way of the pagans, seemed easier, better, and more alluring. While not losing their faith in the saving power of Yahweh, they went off to seek other lovers.

This Covenant relationship between Yahweh and Israel is beautifully described in the Old Testament in the book of the Prophet Hosea. God presents himself as the rejected lover and Israel is compared to an unfaithful and ungrateful wife.

"When Israel was a child I loved him, out of Egypt I called my son. The more I called them, the farther they went from me, Sacrificing to the Baals; and burning incense to idols. Yet it was I who taught Ephraim to walk, who took them in my arms; I drew them with human cords, with bands of love; I fostered them like one who raises an infant to his cheeks; yet, though I stooped to feed my child, they did not know that I was their healer." (Hosea 11.1-4)

The tragedy is as simple as the Bible records it: God loved Israel as a father loves his child; He entered into a covenant with her as a husband enters into a sacred covenant with his wife. Yet Israel chose to play the harlot (Hosea 4 and 5). She accepted the Law of the Lord, but did not live it.

"There is no fidelity, no mercy, no knowledge of God in the land. False swearing, lying, murder, stealing and adultery! in their lawlessness, bloodshed follows bloodshed." (Hosea 4.1-2)

Another Prophet, Amos, stressed the injustice and formalism in Israel's life. ". . . they [Israel] sell the just man for silver, and the poor man for a pair of sandals. They trample the heads of the weak into the dust of the earth, and force the lowly out of the way." (Amos 2.6-7)

"I hate, I despise your feasts, and I take no delight in your solemn assemblies. Even though you offer me your burnt offerings and cereal offerings, I will not accept them. . . . Take away from me the noise of your songs; to the melody of your harps I will not listen. But let justice roll down like waters, and righteousness like an ever-flowing stream." (Amos 5.21-24)

71

If God were all-powerful, could He not have found an easier way? Yet God respects His own creation; He respects man and works through man. He does not suppress the laws of human growth. He started with mankind where mankind was and proceeded from there.

Through Crisis to Readiness

God tried to spare His people from His punishing hand. He gave them a conscience in the voice of the Prophets. They refused to listen to God's call to return to His way. Punishment had to come.

The conscience of Israel spoke. Its judgment came from such strong and varied personalities as the betrayed husband Hosea, the rustic Amos, the enthusiastic Ezekiel, the poet Isaiah, and the timid and faltering Jeremiah. Their loud and clear voices condemned bribery, adultery, lack of social justice, and meaningless ceremonials.

Nevertheless, the Israelites rejected the conscience that was intended to lead them towards fulfillment of the Covenant. Punishment was inevitable and came in the form of the exile. Yet even this will later be seen as part of the preparation of the new and final age.

When the Israelites were driven into exile and stripped of their confidence in the Covenant, the idea of salvation began to deepen and to expand. Even in the physical order, crisis is the beginning of recovery, of a new beginning. In the same manner, Israel began to penetrate the deeper mystery of God's saving power. She began to realize that the saving power and will of Yahweh would be exhibited in a manner that exceeds even the greatness of His saving deeds of the Exodus. The new salvation will be so great, that it will be equivalent to a new creation. It will be new, the final, the eternal salvation (cf. Jeremiah 23.6; 33.16; Zechariah 9.9; Isaiah 45.7; 51.6).

Salvation came to signify a new Zion, a new Israel, a new revelation of the character of Yahweh and, by implication, a new world (Ezekiel 36.29; 37.23).

The great crisis of Israel's adolescence had passed. Through its suffering, failures, longings, and disappointments, Israel came to realize that there must be a lot more to life than mere power and material possessions. Israel was ready; the fullness of time had come for the final and definitive stage of God's plan.

chapter five

From Death to Life: The Christ Event

The Phenomenon of Christ

One of the great phenomena of our world today is that, "over an appreciable region of the earth, a zone of thought has appeared and grown in which a genuine universal love has not only been conceived and preached, but has been shown to be psychologically possible and operative. . . ."[1] This phenomenon should be of special interest to science today since this movement of universal love seems to be gaining in speed and intensity. In fact, a casual judgment of the observable effects of this movement seems to warrant giving it the characteristics of a new phylum in the development of life. There is in this movement the appearance of a specifically new state of life, Christian Love — foolishness to those who have not experienced it.

In the Christian phenomenon, we are aware of thousands of men and women living today who possess a burning zeal, a passionate fervor that outstrips by far in brightness and purity the devotion of any human love. When such a large portion of our world still lives by the philosophy of the survival of the fittest, we marvel to find these thousands of dedicated Christians

74

from different backgrounds and nationalities giving of themselves without limitation to their fellowmen. Whether it is the missioner operating a nutrition clinic in North India or the interested person working with the gangs in the slums of some large U.S. city, many, from the ranks of the rich and the poor, the educated and uneducated, the skilled and the unskilled, have discovered in "the way" a new life of fulfillment through giving.

What is this great love that has produced not only Teresa of Avila, Ignatius of Loyola, Francis of Assisi, John XXIII, Martin Luther King, John and Robert Kennedy, Dietrich Bonhoeffer, but also the thousands of nameless giants of love who have dedicated themselves to a life of faith and conviction? If the transforming love of God that burns in the hearts of these faithful were extinguished, the enormous edifice of rites, of hierarchy, and of doctrines that comprise the Church would revert to the dust from which it arose.[2]

Yet even in these giants of Christian living, there is still the combination of the selfish with the unselfish. To know what basically constitutes the Christian phenomenon, it is important to try to see it in its purest and most developed form.

We have one pure example that can give us the true substance of the Christian phenomenon: the living person of Jesus Christ, "that mystery hidden from ages and generations . . . Christ in you, your hope of glory." (Colossians 1.26f.)

In a way we are at a disadvantage, since there is no exact biography about this man and no exact history book about His life. Yet we know Him through the eyes of His followers, who first experienced the transforming power of this man and reflected deeply on the meaning of His words, deeds, and life. They were not interested in recording cold, statistical facts, but in attempting to bring out the inner unity and meaning of the Christ-event as they experienced it.

The mystery of Jesus of Nazareth is paradoxical. Hated and crucified, He was unknown by the historians of His day; yet, He has outlived all. With a strange persistence His influence endures today. He still haunts the minds of men as His power remains incomprehensible and mysterious. The power of His Spirit grows from day to day. Christ still challenges and disturbs us as no other conqueror or creator has ever done.

Pharaoh built great pyramids, lasting monuments of dead stone. Caesar was famous in the time of Jesus and conquered great lands. Plato was revered throughout the Greek world. People still discuss the Pharaohs, the Roman rulers, and the great philosophers of the past, but who looks to Caesar for security, and who, besides a professor of history or philosophy, becomes zealous about Plato? On the contrary, Christ is still living among us. There are people today who love Him, and there are people who hate Him; there is still a passion for the love of Christ and a passion for His destruction. Some oppose Him directly, others try to discredit Him. Still others try to laugh Him off as a psychological crutch.

Could all this attention not be a proof, or at least an indication, that He is not dead but continues to live and work among us? There is the dynamic joy of those who say they have found Him. There is the deep frustration of many who are not conscious of Him.

The Old Testament is a tutor charged with leading us to Christ. In preparation for the new creation, the faithful remnant of the Old Testament provided the final endometrium of the womb of mother earth, into which the seed of the new creation would be implanted.

The preparation for the new creation reached its culminating point in Mary. Her immediate, docile response initiated the final stage in the development of mankind. "She conceived of the Holy Spirit. . . . And the Word was made flesh and dwelt among us." He immersed Himself in the world by becoming a tiny particle in the world. Then from this point, from the very heart of the matter, He assumes the control and leadership of what we now call evolution.[3] Emptying Himself of His divinity (Philippians 2.5-11), Christ unites Himself with the flesh of the world to unite the world with God. By this He will purify the world and bring it to fulfillment.

In the fullness of time when all things were ready, in the same majestic silence as the other great moments of the world, God took on flesh. This journey of God from the everlasting into the transitory — this leap into human history — is something no human intellect can comprehend. If the mystery of God is difficult, the mystery of the Incarnation is even more difficult. We are now face-to-face not only with God, but with the God-man. The mystery of the Incarnation involves both the mystery of God and the mystery of Man.

Here we stand at the very threshold of the trouble of so many who can easily accept the divine Christ, but are still scandalized by the human Christ. They still cannot see that Christ became like us in all things save sin. Yet because He took on flesh, he had to suffer the effects of sin. Christ the God-man is not a literary form; he is literal truth.

Can Mysteries be Explained?

How can we begin to explain the mystery of a man who suffered the greatest human failure in the history of mankind, and whose power grows daily through this failure? Christ's power is not an external power, but a transforming one that does not destroy. It is the power that penetrates to the heart, and nurtures the dynamic and creative power of human love. This is the mystery of the seemingly naive Lover who dies on Calvary because He loves His fellowmen. "The message of the cross is complete absurdity to those who are headed for ruin, but to us who are experiencing salvation it is the power of God. . . . Yes, Jews demand 'signs' and Greeks look for 'wisdom,' but we preach Christ crucified — a stumbling block to Jews, and an absurdity to Gentiles; but to those who are called, Jews and Greeks alike, Christ the power of God and the wisdom of God." (1 Corinthians 1.18, 22-24)

What is in this man that made Christ greater than His death? What is this transforming power in Him that has arisen again and again after attempted burials of His influence? Consider the age of the Enlightenment, the rise of Rationalism, or the spread of Communism. Try to find a rational answer to this fascinating question. (See 1 Corinthians 1.18-25.)

The more we penetrate into the meaning of this mystery, the more we discover that human logic, reason, philosophy, or wisdom alone can never give an explanation. This does not mean this mystery is something irrational or contrary to human understanding. We know in our own lives that our hearts have reasons that reason itself cannot reason to. The heart might be said to be suprarational. This is also true with the mystery of Christ. It is the story of the Lover that toppled humanly constructed values by transcending them. Only along this line of thinking will we be able to come to the ultimate meaning of the mystery of Jesus of Nazareth.

People have made the grave mistake of trying to understand this supreme mystery by reducing it to truths expressed by definitions. The truth that is Jesus is so rich that definition almost destroys it. Only by constant suggestion that will lead men to explore deeper and deeper will we be able to reach the Christ-event. The person of Christ is the fullness of truth. In Him truth is incarnated. Statements can be made about Him, dogmatic definitions can be deduced from His teaching and example, and His message can be presented in simple propositions. Nevertheless, no human formulation, no matter how orthodox and correct it may be, can exhaust the totality of Jesus.

It is not just His words or His message that constitutes the fullness of truth, but the person of Jesus. The experience of encountering Him cannot possibly be reduced to words. The words that represent religious experience must be symbols, not circumscriptions. They must be more like signals on the mountaintops than warning signals on the road. The words must inspire, stimulate, and urge a person to keep on seeking. So few people really appreciate how subtle and far-reaching the mystery of Jesus is because we have allowed this mystery to be enclosed in sterile concepts. These might be orthodox, definite, and clear but they are as stimulating and nourishing as the plastic bag that contains food.

People have attempted to cramp spiritual fact into formalized abstractions. In trying to define and clarify, they have often succeeded only in veiling the living reality with cold, formal words. In Jesus there came to the sphere of human experience a spiritual force of such beauty, strength, and warmth that those who have felt it find that the only language adequate to describe it is, "God is Love."

It is characteristic of love that it cannot be expressed in

mere words. This is probably why love is best expressed verbally through poetry, for poetry suggests far more that it actually says. Poetry does not attempt to capture the meaning of events through words in a restricted sense; rather it seeks to point to the deeper significance of events that words alone can never define.

The same applies to the life of Jesus. His life suggests far more than His words could say, and that is why so many have tried and failed to understand the real meaning of Jesus. Theologians who have tried to explain in cold words and philosophical systems the Incarnation and Redemption can never adequately express the mystery of the Christ-event.

Philosophers and theologians tried to treat the limitless depth and beauty of the Christ-event as though it were carthorse to be harnessed between the shafts of their ideas: Augustinian, Scholastic, Existentialist, Teilhardian, or any other. No system can harness the wealth and depth of the God who became fully man. Creeds and theologies are only valuable symbols that summarize yet point to a far greater reality. Although these symbols explain the Christian Message, they should be seen more as indicators pointing to the depths of faith that articulation cannot penetrate.

Beginnings

Even a casual reading of the Gospels shows how the Christian community captured the transforming power of Jesus. The poet takes the simple, everyday syllables of language, and Jesus also took the simple, everyday elements of life: soil, the seed, water, work, rest, and found a place for them in His message. Through Him the elements of life become notes and chords in a new symphony. He took people

80

just as they were: the tax-collector receiving bribes, the crusted, cursing, stinking fishermen, or the clean-cut young man — sinners or saints.

He helped men find the beauty, joy, and strength of unfailing love in daily life. So much of life is routine, yet man seeks to have his life lifted up — filled with romance, joy, excitement, and truly with the Spirit. If the hunger for fulfillment has an answer, could not the answer be that there is one in whom seemingly disjointed things attain their unity, one through whom insignificant things begin to fit into the cadence of something greater? In truth it is the Master who gives Life to life. It is the Son of God who brings to life that poetry by which purpose and meaning are once again attuned to God.

The early Christian community pictured Christ as one "who was tempted in every way that we are, yet never sinned . . . who is able to deal patiently with erring sinners, for he himself also is beset by weakness, and by reason thereof is obliged to offer for sins." (Hebrew 4.15; 5.2f.) The more primitive catechesis of the early community pictures the man Jesus accepting a humanity — our humanity — burdened with the constant temptations of escape and power.

The Gospels picture the beginning of the public ministry of Jesus with the temptations. Temptations come throughout His life, reaching their high point in the Agony in the garden. The temptations described in the Gospels are those that plague all men. They were the temptations Christ accepted when He became man.

The record of the temptations is highly symbolic. The elements of Jesus' inner struggle are projected like figures in a drama. The voice that whispered in His inner being becomes eternalized. Temptations become personified in the tempter.

The message comes through clearly. Humanity was the battlefield on which Jesus was to proclaim and fight His revolution. Let us consider more closely the message of these temptations. (See Luke 4.1-12.)

"Command this stone to turn into bread." Jesus knew how hard men had to work and how little they received for their work. He had experienced the urgency of the needs of the masses who merely existed. Christ also realized that, in one way, the poor were better off because they realized they were in need. The wealthy thought they had everything. For them, food, drink, and games were life. How could anyone speak to the rich of something they needed when they were convinced they had everything?

Christ lightened the burden of His brethren. He showed them the way by offering something new to the over-taxed and under-rewarded people. Was the solution giving them money and free food? Is this the solution to our poverty problems today? Should countries just become welfare states, giving out free food, medicines, and clothing? Wouldn't this perpetuate the original fault by helping man to escape his responsibility for the development of the world? Christ's mission was not to be a welfare worker, but to show men how to turn their meager existence into the fullness of life. I am sure that Jesus was constantly tempted to simply give the people the material goods they lacked. It would have been so easy, but it would eventually have reduced them to the level of pets.

Jesus knew that within the hearts of humans an infinite hunger exists that no material things can satisfy. As long as people seek only material things, they will never truly live. This hunger for human fulfillment is quickened and must be fed.

Jesus answers, "Not by bread alone shall man live." Jesus does not deny the necessity of material things; they are part of God's gift to man and are to be used and enjoyed. However, the response is clear — "not by bread alone." It is true that material things are good and necessary for life, but by themselves they can never be sufficient for true and lasting happiness. While we can enjoy a good meal and savor delicate wine, we all realize that eating, drinking, and other sensual pleasures are not sufficient for human fulfillment. If we live only through the senses, the senses become corrupted — the more they receive, the more they will demand and the less they will be satisfied. The message of Jesus proclaims from the beginning that while material things are good and necessary, there is a lot more to life than material goods.

"I will give you power and glory." Today, as in days past, this continues to be one of the great temptations of many businessmen who seek to control more and more, of parents who insist on running Junior's life even though he is grown-up, of nations that impose their forms of government on other nations. We want to be able to impose our ideas and way of life on others. "If you worship before me, the whole world shall be yours." This is the temptation of the unprincipled man who will do anything to attain his end.

Jesus came to bring about a reversal of values. The wisdom and glory of the world that was leading the world to destruction had to be exchanged for the wisdom of God if man was to be united with God. How was Christ to lead people to become more human through the guidance of the Spirit rather than more animal-like through slavery to the flesh?

Jesus had to risk failure because He lived and ventured on a scale that would take the development of the ages to express fully. To win the world would be nothing without having won the hearts of man. "You shall worship the Lord your God, and him only shall you serve." (Luke 4.8) Although the temptations of worldly wisdom were most alluring, Jesus remained faithful to proclaim the true wisdom of God, so that believing we now may have life. He chose to proclaim the truth rather than to win popularity. He chose to be the Suffering Servant rather than the powerful King-Messiah. His goal was to rule from within the hearts of man rather than by external forces and punitive laws.

"Throw yourself down from here . . . for the angels will preserve you." This is the great temptation of the average good man. The Satan within us seems to say, "So, you think you have won; well, I will show you just how weak and ridiculous you are!" Jesus chose the way of faithfulness to the Father. Surely God would protect His Son with His favor. What surer evidence of faith could there be than to trust in God's constant favor?

Isn't this the temptation many of us fall into frequently, perhaps without realizing it? "I've given myself to God and He will protect me." Or, "I go to Mass and Communion on Sundays and contribute to the support of the Church. Why should I get involved in the suffering and misery of migrant workers in South Texas or grapepickers in California?" This is a constant temptation: to escape from the responsibilities of being human and seclude ourselves within the confines of a magic religion, expecting too much of God and too little of man. A false trust in God is based on a false understanding of the Covenant relationship. Israel remembered that God had promised protection, but forgot that they had promised fidelity to the Covenant.

This is the temptation of the good man. It is an even greater temptation for the average good religious. "I've got nothing to worry about: God will take care of things." Many so-called good people fail to realize that conversion to Christ is conversion to His way of life. It calls for unceasing growth in Him. We are always in a process of conversion until the moment of our final and irreversible conversion, our passing into the fullness of life.

Christ knew human nature. He knew that habits and customs that were the product of generations would not be easily changed. His task was to awaken in man the need for turning to God daily. "Give us this day our daily bread." It is not easy to trust with complete confidence, but the more a child experiences the loving care of his father, the more he will learn to be trusting. Yet the temptation to abuse this trust will always be with us.

After the devil had tried every temptation, he departed for a while. At many moments of His life, Jesus had to face the same temptations. So it is with us. Many times in life, sometimes daily, we have to face temptations; we have to choose between my way or God's way, the easy way out or the true way, the way of loveless humanity or the way of loving man.

Having accepted the world Christ was ready to start His mission. Christ entered the arena of human life as an idealist of infinitely high hopes who never for a moment lost sight of the real world of flesh and blood.

Heralding the New Creation

The stage was prepared by the Old Testament. The Gospel writers were ready to begin their presentation of the Word made Flesh. They described Jesus' proclamations that the Kingdom of God was at hand. (Matthew 4.17; Mark 1.14-15; Luke 4.18-22; 4.43) The long-awaited Kingdom of peace, joy, justice, productivity, and equality had begun. (See Jeremiah 31.31-34; Hosea 2.14-23; Ezekiel 37.21-28; Isaiah 42.1-7; 49.1-6; 50.4-9; 52.13-53.12.) The full significance of this new Kingdom would become clear only with the Christ-event. It would include all the events of Jesus' life, culminating in His death and resurrection. The new Kingdom of Yahweh and observance of His Law would not be given from some external source. It would be written in the hearts of men (Jeremiah 31.33-34). The Kingdom would be the new relationship between Yahweh and the people, based on the tender love and mercy of Yahweh and the faithfulness of the people (Hosea 3.1ff.).

The Jews of Christ's time associated Kingdom with one similar to David, but the Kingdom of God was to be far greater than any political kingdom. It could never be achieved through political activity alone, nor would it come about through force, for force denies love and freedom. The new Kingdom would come through the depth of the riches of God's wisdom (Romans 11.33). It would appear as foolishness next to the wisdom of the world. Yet the foolishness of God is greater than man's wisdom, and the weakness of God is greater than man's might (1 Corinthians 1.18-25). It would go directly to the heart of man. Touched by this new power, acknowledging and accepting it, man would begin a new life. The new creation would emerge from within.

At first Christ announced the Kingdom proclaimed by the Prophets and expected by the people. He knew that the notions of the people about the Kingdom were inadequate and

86

confused. But this was the world into which He had come, so He had to begin there. Without complaining, as some reformers do today, that much of what the people believed was wrong and to be forgotten, Jesus appealed to them with true notions of the Kingdom.

The Kingdom of God was to be a Kingdom of peace. But peace did not mean a simple, passive attitude. Our modern idea of peace is inadequate for expressing the biblical concept of shalom. Shalom is a condition of personal and community life broader than the mere absence of armed conflict, and far richer than peace of mind or peace of soul. It is a dynamic condition of peace, joy, and human reciprocity that comes from true human freedom and responsibility, social harmony, and exalted justice. It signifies abundance of crops, good health, and most of all, true fellowship among men. Shalom indicates the fullness of a truly integrated life, both personal and social, resulting in a great joy and gladness. Shalom would be characteristic of the Kingdom of love.

The Prince of Peace, who was to bring about an ever-increasing Kingdom of justice and peace, was foretold by Isaiah (9.2-7). When He finally came into the world He was announced with the greeting, "peace on earth" (Luke 2.14). The long-awaited Kingdom of peace, of justice, and of love was at hand. Jesus would proclaim this through every transforming deed and word.

Jesus chose the ordinary expressions of everyday life to reveal His message. He compared the Kingdom to the sower and the seed that falls on the ground; to the wheat that grows with the weeds; to the mustard seed; to the leaven mixed with the flour; to a great treasurer; to a great pearl; to a net that gathers all kinds of fish. Jesus did not give clear-cut dogmatic definitions of the Kingdom. He gave His listeners lessons on the Kingdom that described rather than defined, that opened up new possibilities rather than shut off further thought and reflection. Christ led them to discover for themselves. Yet, in all these lessons, three characteristics stood out: growth from within, a certain greatness, and a mixture of all kinds of people in the Kingdom here on earth.

In time, Jesus began to explain the inner nature of the Kingdom. "But whoever drinks the water I give him, will never be thirsty; no, the water I give shall become a fountain within him, leaping up to provide eternal life." (John 4.14) "I myself am the bread of life. No one who comes to me shall ever be hungry, no one who believes in me shall ever thirst." (John 6.35) "Love your enemies, do good to those who hate you; bless those who curse you and pray for those who maltreat you. Give to all who beg from you." (Luke 6.27-28, 30) Not everyone who says "Lord, Lord, will enter the Kingdom of God but only the one who does the will of my Father in Heaven." (See Matthew 5.1-7.29 for Jesus' explication of this.) The people asked Him, "Sir, give us this bread always." (John 6.34) But as Jesus gave them more and more of Himself, the Bread of Life, they began to depart with the words, "This is a hard saying: Who can listen to it?"

Jesus was not naively talking about "peace" and "love." He was a realist who knew too well the corrupting sinfulness of mankind. He knew how man had rejected God's invitation to share in His creative activity of developing the world. Jesus spoke about love, patience, and understanding, but He also brought out forcefully the idea of stewardship. One of the frequent characters in the Gospel is the steward, the man who has responsibility and exercises the power assigned to him by his master. The lazy and irresponsible steward who hides his money in the earth, or beats the servants in the master's absence is rebuked by Jesus. Paul continued this theme when he described the Christian as an heir who puts away childhood dependencies, assumes the duties of an adult, and becomes responsible for his father's estate.

Jesus more subtly showed man's responsibility for the creative activity of the universe through His miracles. Many people see in the miracles of Jesus simply an apologetic proof for His mission, but the miracles mean far more than that. The Bible sees the beginning of evil in man's refusal to take his place as the true lord of the world. Through his sin, man released evil powers, pictured by primitive people as demons. These powers of greed, selfishness, laziness, hatred, and revenge succeeded in corrupting both man and his world. As Paul put it, "Creation was made subject to futility, not of its own accord [nature] but by him [man] who once subjected it; yet not without hope, because the world itself will be freed from its slavery to corruption and share in the glorious freedom of the children of God. For we know that all creation groans and travails in pain until now." (Romans 8.19-22)

What does this have to do with the meaning of the miracles performed by Jesus? The synoptics used the term power, while John used the term sign for miracle. This power or sign was always related to the central mystery of the Gospel, the person of Jesus. With Jesus, God's power erupted among men. Even Jesus' contemporaries understood this eruption as something definitive. Power in the Gospels suggested that something was being defeated — the power of evil. When the Gospels speak of Jesus' power, they often mention that He was full of indignation.

Why would He be indignant at using His power to cure the leper (Mark 1.41), or to calm the storm (Mark 4.39-40)? Why is Jesus pictured as almost battling with the evil demons (Mark 1.25-27)?

In Jesus, the struggle between the destructive powers of evil and the creative powers of good was coming to a climax. God was completing His creative activity in a final, definitive way. Jesus brought about a new creation. In Mark (7.37), the bystanders note "He has done everything well." Why then would Christ be indignant? Because Jesus was making up for man's laziness, indecision, and lack of responsibility; He was fighting against the powers, injustice, irresponsibility, and egotism that were actively destroying man and his world. Jesus conceived the Kingdom as a Kingdom of love and fellowship, of peace and prosperity, of work and development, of justice and mercy. The miracles were signs of the new Kingdom initiated in the person of Jesus.

The Meaning of Christ's Message

With the beginning of this Kingdom, mankind took on a new role that can be expressed very simply. Man, the world is yours. You have now come of age; take over. Seek to develop the whole world. Develop a whole person who can work, play, cry, laugh, become excited about life, and suffer disappointment. The person who learns to become fully himself finds the key to the Christian Message. In this point, the Gospel and depth psychology are united. Man will find the fullness of life only through an authentic, mature human love expressed by the giving of self to others.

The work of the Lord continues today, in the farmer who cultivates his crops, not only to make a living for his family, but also to produce more food for others; in the business executive who, conscious of his obligations to his workers and the general public, seeks to produce better products; in the experimental chemist who devotes his life to searching for better living through science; in the educator who seeks to provide youth with the learning necessary for total development. They all manifest the Christian Message that says, take the world seriously, develop it, use it, improve it, and remain its master in order to serve your brothers. Never allow the world to become the master of man.

The Kingdom of God is the community of lovers, people who have come to life through faith in Jesus. It is the community held together through the mysterious bonds of love, in constant hope-put-into-action of better things to come. Through the dedication and work of men of good will, the Kingdom of God is coming more and more into existence. A true Christian cannot be anything but an optimist.

How can this love come about? Will it be instantaneous? Far from it. Faith is only the beginning. Because we are of the flesh, laziness, sensuality, greed, and egotism are part of us. Jesus began to explain the meaning of His message by showing the new way to the fullness of life. He tells us to love our enemies, do not get angry, be simple in speech, offer generosity in place of revenge, give alms, pray, avoid judgments, and correct ourselves first before we correct others. Many who hear the words of Jesus will react with distaste. Yet our acceptance must be the acceptance of a child (Luke 18.17) who is told to take some caster oil or a shot of penicillin. He does not like it, but he takes it because he knows it is good for him and that his father would not lie to him.

The demands of Jesus are difficult. It is better to feel distaste for His message and oppose His demands openly than to accept His words unthinkingly as pious platitudes useful for meditation but for nothing else. That is the last thing they are. They are words to shake the very foundations of the world, to bring forth a new creation. The demands are difficult, but we can take comfort in knowing that we are not alone. We "joyfully give thanks to the Father, who has made us capable to become partakers of the lot of the saints." (Colossians 1.11-12)

Some may ask if God is a sadist in demanding of men such a seemingly impossible task. Does God enjoy seeing us struggle and suffer? No! He sent His Son into the world that we might live. It is precisely because humanity had perverted itself by its own ingenuity and wisdom that the conversion must be difficult. It is man who produced the spark that eventually grew into the great bonfire of evil. The merciful Father sent His Son to put out the fire of evil, and to administer the cure that will lead men to the fullness of life.

Jesus summarized the essence of His message by saying: "Whoever wishes to be my follower must deny his very self, take up his cross each day and follow in my steps. Whoever would save his life will lose it and whoever loses his life for my sake will save it." (Luke 9.23-24) What will following this involve? Forget yourself and you will find life. Give yourself to others and you will find yourself. Stop being egotistical and allow your true self to blossom forth. This process of self-giving will involve failure, disappointments, loneliness, frustration, and rejection, but in the long run, it will nurture that authentic inner joy of the true Christian.

To the faithless mind, the message of Jesus is not difficult; it is impossible! How can Jesus be followed when He asks things so contrary to our common way of acting? One of the great troubles of contemporary Christianity is that so many Christians, rather than converting themselves to Christianity, have converted Christianity to their way of life. This is the challenge to existential man. Man's boundless possibilities is revealed most clearly in his calling to supplant ordinary sin-damaged life with new life in Jesus. Rising above the ordinary inhibitions of sinful humanity, people will begin to move on the level of a fully authentic human freedom. That freedom reflecting the nature of the divine, we will come to share more and more in the mind and Spirit of the Father.

The man of Nazareth did not simply proclaim a message; His own life was a living example of the new way He proclaimed. The Gospels are full of examples showing how Jesus not only preached but also lived to the fullest what He preached. He totally forgot Himself in working for the needs of others, often to the point of exhaustion. Jesus was so tired that He slept in the midst of a great storm. He was exhausted and hungry in Samaria. He suffered great anguish in the final Agony of the garden (Luke 22.39ff.). But his sufferings did not diminish His sense of mission. He had compassion for the widow whose only son had died. He loved His friends Mary, Martha, and Lazarus. He relieved many of their afflictions. He consoled all who received Him in their hearts.

The message of Jesus is today confirmed by depth psychology. In fact, some psychologists claim that depth psychology is the best positive apologetic for Christianity. Man cannot find fulfillment in himself, but in relation to others. The more he opens himself and gives himself to others, the more he will find himself. The biblical concept of salvation gained by losing one's life would be psychologically explained as wholeness.

Depth psychology knows no better way to express fulfillment than through these concepts. Psychology confirms that the most basic need of man is to love. Authentic love is a gift of self for the good of the other. The more we give in this way, the more we shall be fulfilled. The more we annihilate ourselves, the more our whole self will emerge.[4]

Lord, Teach Us to Pray

One important element we cannot overlook in the example Jesus gave us is the necessity of prayer. In the past the emphasis tended to be on the vertical — God coming to man in revelation and man responding to God in faith. In recent times the stress is changing to seek God in the horizontal — in and through our fellowmen. Some today say the days of prayer to the Father are over. We have come of age, so that we meet God only in fellowship with others.

Jesus is usually pictured with the disciples, the crowds, or His friends. Yet Jesus is a man of prayer. He prayed in solitude (Mark 1.35; Luke 5.16). He prayed before each important step in His life: at His Baptism (Luke 3.21); before the choice of the Twelve (Luke 6.12); before the final decision to be subjected to the cross (Mark 14.32-42). He prayed at the end of a long day's work (Matthew 14.23).

Today when so many are drifting away from reflective prayer, non-Christian philosophers, such as Erich Fromm (see "The Art of Loving"), insist that people need a disciplined, daily period of reflection if they are going to be capable of loving.

Recently at an airport, I picked up a copy of a book on psychocybernetics. One of the things that struck me while paging through the book was its insistence on a daily period of reflection as an absolute condition for personal success. It is a little amusing that man is finally discovering on his own what Jesus made known to us two thousand years ago. Each of us has a need to be alone, to look into ourselves, to reflect, to hear the beat of our heart. Only with God will we be able to discover our true role and mission in life. The true self, emerging through interaction with community life, will become known in the solitude of personal reflection.

The Christian today, who knows that every good work done out of charity is also a prayer, may be somewhat surprised to discover how many times Jesus, who is love incarnate, withdrew to pray. In Mark's Gospel we see how, after a night of prayer, Jesus realizes still more profoundly what His real task is, where His true service to man lies (see Mark 1.35-38). "It is through prayer that the compass which directs our activities remains true."[5]

Through Death to the New Creation

Christ's final days are the ones most familiar to most of us. The Last Supper, His perpetual gift of self in the Eucharist, preceded His arrest. He knew that the hour had come. During His life He had experienced how sin hardens men's hearts and closes their eyes, ears, and hearts to the truth. He spoke to them in parables and with unequivocal words. The example of His life had only hardened them more, as His words were in effect a condemnation of their lives. People had to condemn Christ to justify themselves (Matthew 12.24; Luke 11.15 ff. Mark 3.22 ff.). Do we not often do the same in our lives? When someone speaks words that might cause us to reexamine our lives, do we seek to discredit him rather than to see if there might be some element of truth in what he says?

When the hour came for the final round, the power of evil met in a head-on clash with the power of the Spirit." . . . He humbled himself, obediently accepting even death, death on a cross." (Philippians 2.8) Christ came on a mission from the Father to free man from his self-imposed bondage of sin. He proclaimed the message, explained it, and lived it. Sinful humanity closed its eyes, ears, and hearts to the message of redemption. Jesus had to take the final step. He freely gave His life that we might live. The supreme act of obedience to the Father's will to save man was His complete and unselfish love for man. "There is no greater love than this: to lay down one's life for one's friends." (John 15.13)

The Gospels are filled with expressions that show that Jesus was not forced to die, but freely accepted death as the final price. He accepted the sins of humanity (Isaiah 52.13-53.12); He took unto Himself flesh, and allowed His body to be put to death that He might put a decisive end to the reign of evil. Christ, the new Adam, inaugurated a new era of the Spirit by allowing His body to be crucified. He had taken upon Himself the sin of the world, although He never gave in to sin. Sinful humanity, in its blindness, would seek to destroy Him. The hour for the final battle had arrived.

The narratives of the Passion and Death portray Jesus in perfect control of the situation. He allowed Himself to be arrested (John 18.4-9). He suffered deeply, yet never lost control. Jesus knew His mission; He freely accepted it. He was responsible for the salvation of man, and did not give up when the going got tough. The deep physical and mental sufferings of Jesus during His final hours are a vivid description of the products of evil. The selfishness, egotism, escapism, and greed of humanity lead to His Passion and Death.

John portrays beautifully how Jesus ascended the cross in triumph. Jesus' triumph was not easy, and offered no masochistic pleasure. It was the victorious climax to His battle against evil. Yet, to all appearances, the powers of evil had triumphed. They had succeeded in destroying the spirit of love. In the eyes of the world, Jesus had failed. He had given it a good try, but the poor man had failed. He was defeated by His enemies. But let us penetrate more deeply into what is hidden in the death of Jesus on the cross.

"Jesus, uttering a loud cry, breathed his last." (Mark 15.37) It was unusual to die on the cross with a loud cry. Somebody who was crucified usually passed quietly from complete exhaustion. It was so extraordinary that Mark records, "The centurion who stood guard over him, on seeing the manner of his death, declared, 'Clearly this man was the Son of God.' " (Mark 15.39) Roman centurions were hardened men used to seeing death by the cross. What then was so unusual in Christ's crucifixion? Remembering the hatred and the mockeries of the Jewish authorities, the centurion knew who really won. In his pagan way, he recognized divine power rested in Jesus, and not in the Jews. His was probably a true expression of faith in the Son of God. Even if it were a purely pagan observation, it was the exclamation of one who had witnessed an awe-inspiring death.

None of the evangelists, in narrating Christ's crucifixion, used the word "died." This was said only by outsiders who did not believe (Mark 15.44). Mark simply says Jesus expired. The other evangelists bring out even more clearly the full impact. "Once again Jesus cried out in a loud voice, and then gave up his spirit." (Matthew 27.50) "Jesus uttered a loud cry and said, 'Father, into your hands I commend my spirit.' After he said this, he expired." (Luke 23.46) "When Jesus had received the vinegar, he said, 'It is finished'; and he bowed his head and gave up his spirit." (John 19.30) What is to be made of all this?

The evangelists wished to stress the personal character of Jesus' death. Jesus was not killed; His life was not taken from Him. He gave His life out of His own free will. This act of free obedience and love is the basis of our redemption.

Jesus ascended the cross triumphantly, as it was there that He brought forth the new creation by giving up His spirit (John 19.30) and by permitting blood and water to flow from His side (John 19.34). We are reminded of the beginning of time, when the Spirit of God hovered over the waters and directed the work of creation. John, who constantly spoke of Jesus as the new Moses, saw in water the sign of the saving activity of the Spirit (e.g.: The crossing of the Red Sea, the sweet drinking water in the desert, and the Baptism of Jesus). Likewise, it was through the blood of the covenant that the people of Israel has been united to God in His saving act.

In His moment of triumph Christ handed over the dynamic, creating Spirit of love that had been driven from the world through man's sinfulness. The destructive spirit of evil was conquered and the creative Spirit of good was released. Once again the Spirit of God was "moving over the face of the waters" (Genesis 1.2). Through the blood of Christ, humanity was united to the Father in a New Covenant.

A man of flesh and blood, Jesus was like us. Yet unlike us He did not run away from real life. He did not pretend to be something He was not; He did not break down when things went badly. He faced reality squarely. Christ knew where He was going and anticipated the consequences. He had a mission to accomplish, and He freely accepted His responsibility to both His Father and to humanity. In the end, it was this spirit of love that triumphed over the spirit of evil. Love alone can be truly victorious. This was Christ's message, and He lived it till the end, which was, in reality, the beginning of a new creation. Christ invited humanity, "Come, follow me."

In order to understand correctly the meaning of our redemption, we must see the entire Christ-event of salvation and redemption as one act: Incarnation-Life-Passion-Resurrection-Pentecost.

I have attempted to present a brief sketch of the meaning of the Christ-event. I feel it is quite inadequate, not only because of my own personal limitations, but also because of the boundless richness of the Christ-event. It is only through study, reflection, and prayer that we come gradually to appreciate the full impact of what Christ has done. The Christ-event becomes even more meaningful when we consider that this God-man, who through death entered into life, is inviting us today, through the cross, to enter into the fullness of life. Christ triumphed over the powers of egoism, selfishness, and greed. United with Him, and through Him with others, I live in the confidence that I too am triumphing. Though struggling and falling seven times a day, I am triumphing because He has triumphed.

chapter six

New Creation: 'Christogenesis'

Evolution and Depersonalization

During the past few hundred years, mankind has been progressing at an ever-increasing pace. Within our own lifetime, we have witnessed, with amazement and enjoyment, the results of many discoveries: better dentist drills, better roads, heart transplants, trips to the moon, and instant projection of worldwide events on television. Yet, there is another side to this human story of progress that has caused us much suffering: crime, murder, brutality, and total war. The technology that is meant to fashion a more livable world is also being utilized to more effectively perpetrate crime and destruction.

Some seek to get ahead by imposing their will or way of living upon others. Others seek to keep segments of the population in the darkness of ignorance to be assured of cheap labor. This is an acute problem both in underdeveloped countries and throughout the United States. For instance, in many small towns in Texas, Mexican children are kept from getting a decent education. It is impossible for them to enter college, so they must stay on the farm and work at subhuman wages.

There are many subtle ways in which man is still trying

to get ahead by stepping on the dignity of his fellowmen. Should we then be surprised at riots, the burning of cities, and bloody revolutions? Corner even a friendly animal, and it will be forced to fight. If we beat, take advantage of, enslave, humiliate, and frustrate our fellowman, we eventually will force him to come out fighting. True human progress cannot come about at the expense of people.

Yet, even if progress was being made as fast as it superficially appears to be, and even if there were no abuses or injustice, from the phenomenological point of view something essential is missing. Men have become so involved in their work, whether it is education, chemical research, or business analysis that they have become more like machines and less like men. People seem to forget that machines — IBM computers, electronic calculators — are products of men's ingenuity and were designed to help men in their work. Many people have become slaves to their own instruments, and unconsciously seek to imitate them.

Today many large firms are resorting to professional services to help their staffs become more human. Professional psychologists have been engaged to conduct sensitivity sessions among staff members, with the purpose of affecting better communication. Business is beginning to discover that when man becomes more machinelike and less human, efficiency drops. If for no reason other than making greater profits, corporations are seeking ways of helping their personnel to be more human.

There is another significant aspect in the contemporary trend towards depersonalization. For practical purposes, man is being deprived even of his name. Persons are coded according to social security numbers: "From now on you are 49-6772-

482." Quite a romantic name, isn't it? Have you ever gone through the registration line of a college? or filled out forms for an employment agency? or even filled out a blank to get an IBM computer to line you up with a date? Many of the modern conveniences are depriving man of the unique mystery of his personality. The person, who can be truly known only in relationship, is slowly disappearing, while cold, rational specifications, like those of the computer, are taking his place. There is no warmth, no compassion in such mechanized life. By eliminating the person from the sphere of our experience, we eliminate the very ground of love. It is only a person that is capable of loving and of being loved.

It seems therefore that progress has its problems. What is the answer? Is it to escape to a primitive island in the South Pacific where there are golden beaches, tall palm trees full of coconuts, and cool ocean breezes? The answer can never lie in retreating from progress. We must seek the answer elsewhere, for we are convinced that there is a road for the true and complete progress of man and his world. But where?

The Life Love Gives

Let us each analyze our own experiences. When I do something for others, do I do it because I want to, or because I feel compelled through some external force? Wouldn't it be from love of another? Whether it is the love of husband and wife, the love of parent and child, or friendship, love has the mysterious power that creates the *person* who loves. We cannot explain this adequately in rational terms because we are dealing here with a suprarational phenomenon. We must appeal to experience to understand this essential condition of personal growth. One who has not experienced the transforming and creative power of love is not yet a mature person; he is a human being, but his growth has been stunted.

Look at the young love of a couple first "going steady." The young man begins to take note of his hair, the way he dresses, and the way he acts. How can he please the one who is the object of his admiration? He discovers the answer to be not only by giving her flowers, or rides in his remodeled car, but by creating himself to be a new being: polite, handsome, and fun-loving.

Look at the young couple planning for marriage. The genuineness of their love is shown not by eloping, thinking naively that love will make all things possible, but by working hard to save enough so that together they may make a decent beginning with a place to live. Their coming together in marriage is delayed, not because they do not love one another, but precisely because their mutual love urges them to prepare themselves properly to give themselves to each other. Later on, it is the love for his family that motivates the father to take an extra job, so that he can give more to them.

From my own experience, I should begin to realize that love (or conversely, hate) is the most powerful force at work within me. Freud said all human behavior was somehow related to or motivated by the sexual, but today this is regarded by most psychologists as an oversimplification. We speak of the necessity and value of interpersonal relations, but too many have confused this with sexual relations. Love is something far greater than sex. True love is the greatest of all energies in man. Many times men have endured all kinds of physical and mental torture at the hands of an enemy, but when forced to witness the torturing of one whom they love, they weaken and give in. Even the enemies of love make use of the power of love. Man can muster enough power to allow himself to be tortured to death, but he cannot bear the pains of seeing the same happen to those whom he loves.

The Phylum of Love

True Christian living exhibits all the characteristics of a new category, or phylum, in the tree of life. We have attempted in the previous chapter to show how this new phylum originated; now we want to emphasize how it has been penetrating the world through the ages.

Jesus of Nazareth both preached and lived a true love. He established a personalizing, universal love that was not only psychologically possible, but that was the only complete and final way to truly love. He showed that only through a love that constantly seeks to go beyond oneself to others could the true ego come forth and egotism be destroyed. Christ has shown us how a man is not an authentic human being when he closes in on himself and lives in isolation from others. The truly authentic human being is the loving person. The more one goes out of himself to others, the more he becomes a person. In this way we gradually reach the peak of our originality and uniqueness, our true self.

According to the evolutionary process, each person is a developing microcosmos. Our full person will emerge to the degree that we unite with others through love. Love alone joins people through what is deepest in them. "This is a fact of daily experience. At what moment do lovers come into the most complete possession of themselves if not when they say they are lost in each other? In truth, does not love every instant achieve all around us, in the couple or the team, the magic feat, the feat reputed to be contradictory, of 'personalis-

104

ing' by totalising? And if that is what it can achieve daily on a small scale, why should it not repeat this one day on world-wide dimensions?"[1]

Jesus of Nazareth, the Word made Flesh, took upon Himself the pains of humanity turned in on itself and deprived of the life of love. There was no other way possible for Christ to begin the new order than by immersing Himself in sinful flesh, and accepting death, the natural product of egoism, of man turned in on himself and living the life of death. Through His final gift on the cross, Jesus crucified the flesh and re-leased the Spirit. It is no wonder that the early Church Fathers saw the birth of the Church on the cross. This was a victory through failure. The world was made one by the Creator, but through sin it became divided (Genesis 11.1-9). Once again it was unified through the creative Spirit of the Risen Lord, so that man and his world will work together towards the final perfection.

The final era has begun. Christ died for our sins and rose for our sanctification. Jesus of Nazareth took over the evolution of the world through His presence in all things. The Risen Lord is the new creation in our midst. The Resurrection of Jesus is the irrevocable pledge of man's destiny, the guarantee that man is not lost in a universe of staggering size and distance.

The Early Communities

The community that the Lord began during His earthly life did not disperse after His death. The visible presence of the Risen Lord among His Apostles had prepared them for the final moment when the Holy Spirit was given to them (Luke 24.49; Acts 1.8). Filled with this creative power, the Apostles were able to go forth with the message of salvation. God so loved the world that He gave His only-begotten Son. The Son so loved the world that He gave His life and sent forth His disciples to announce a new energy insuring the development of the world unto perfection and completion.

They did not have any well-developed theologies or creeds, but they did have the living experience of the Lord. Probably the clearest proclamation of His message was the simple command, "Follow me." As the community reflected on the meaning of Jesus, the members continued to imitate as much as possible their life with Him. They had lived together, shared one another's company, and had broken bread together. It was in this relaxed, warm, and personal way that the disciples had come to know the Lord and the transforming power of His love. Their mission was not only to proclaim His words, but to live the beautiful interpersonal life that Christ had introduced to them.

At Pentecost the disciples began to have a full appreciation of the intimate connection between the life of Jesus and the message He proclaimed. (See John 16.12ff.) The experience of living with Him without explicit words would have been ambiguous, while hearing Him without the experience of living with Him would have been futile and empty. It was this lived experience of community that enabled the disciples to understand the energy that would transform the world into a new creation. This energy is summed up in the simple words: "Love one another as I have loved you." (John 15.12) Jesus sent them forth, filled with the Spirit, to call redeemed humanity into the new community of the Children of God.

After the Resurrection, this group that the Lord began continued. The first Christian community could not precisely define itself, but it knew that it was the community of Jesus Christ, Lord. (See Acts 2.32-36; 3.13-15; 10.37-43; 1 Corinthians 15.35.) After Pentecost, the disciples scattered to proclaim the message of new life. Wherever they went, they sought to form other communities that, through faith in the power of the Risen Lord, could hope for better things to come. From the beginning, the ecclesiastical communities never developed in isolation from the mother community at Jerusalem. The new groups were very conscious of an organic growth; the cells were multiplying, but they were all part of the one growing body. There was a rich variety in these developing communities; yet the apparent differences could not conceal the living belief that they were, as Paul puts it so forcefully, the one body of Christ. As the life of Jesus was known by the living of His mission, so the new life of the Spirit would be known by the living of the mission that was entrusted to the disciples by the Risen Lord.

The early Christian community is beautifully described in the Acts of the Apostles (2.42-47; 4.32-35; 5.12-16). It was nourished by the teaching of the Apostles, by the spiritual food of the Eucharist, and by prayer. It is evident throughout the Acts that there was great concern for the teaching of the Apostles. The communities continued to speak and think about the teaching of Jesus as it was transmitted to them by the Apostles. Out of this would eventually come the comparatively fixed body of deeds and teachings of Jesus that would form the source material for the Gospels (cf. Romans 6.17 and 2 Timothy 1.13).

Among the early Christians there was a genuine fellowship of believers. They took to heart the Good News and sincerely strived to live the life of universal charity. They celebrated the breaking of the bread from the very beginning. The basic elements of a liturgy were present: the teaching of the Apostles, the joining in true fellowship, the breaking of bread, and the concluding thanksgiving prayers. This became the model for all future celebrations of the Eucharist. The accidentals will vary with time and place but the essentials initiated by the Lord and practiced by the first communities will always be there.

The life and liturgy of the early Christians were lived with a sense of profound joy and great simplicity (Acts 2.47). Shouldn't this be the guide for our Christian living and liturgical celebrations? Can they be mournful and still be Christian?

The new way was spreading quickly from Jerusalem to Antioch, to Corinth, Ephesus, and to Galatia. A new life, full of promise, prevailed in all these early communities. Despite the many local differences, they were all united through one faith in the Lord Jesus; they shared the Baptism and one Eucharist, heard the same apostolic preaching and instruction, lived together in a spirit of brotherly love, and looked forward to the same eschatological expectation.

Though the first community in Jerusalem is presented in an ideal state, it was characterized by temptations, sufferings and persecutions. One should not be scandalized by the fact that within the community of the redeemed, there is still sin. (The dramatic story of Ananias [Acts 5.1ff.] reflects the sinfulness within the early Christian community.) The community of the Lord began, but it did not reach its final maturity. It was to be a struggling Church on pilgrimage to the Father, and it remains so to this day. The Church's life of holiness will be constantly disfigured by the life of sin of many of its members.

For the early Christians there were no clear-cut tables of organization or detailed constitutions. However, all accepted the existence of an organization in service to the community. The Church was conscious that it was subject to the Glorified Lord who, acting through the Spirit, guides the new people of God to their final completion. All who are entrusted with tasks and services in the Church are simply God's instruments, members of Christ's Risen Body, animated by the same Spirit (1 Corinthians 12.12ff.; Ephesians 2.31; 4.12-16). Those who rule and guide in the name of the Lord are bound, together with all the members, by the same Christian law of service and love that directed the early Church (Mark 10.42-45).

When the community was involved in important decisions, as it was in the dispute over circumcision for the Gentiles (Acts 15.1ff.), the authoritative leadership of the Apostles stands out clearly. Paul gives a well-developed picture of the various functions within a community (1 Corinthians 12.28). The People of God on pilgrimage to the Father are led by human pastors who are responsible for their activity to the principal Shepherd (1 Peter 5.2-4).

The primitive community recognized Simon Peter as chief amongst the Twelve. (Cf. 1 Corinthians 15.5; Luke 24.34, John 21.15-17, with the prominence of Peter's discourse in Acts 1-15). When a point of fundamental importance was involved, Peter decided finally (Acts 15.1ff.).

The early communities were filled with the freedom of the Spirit, but it was the organization of the various ministries within the community that made the new life of the Spirit possible. The order of the communities was not instantly formed, rather it was determined by the members of the community, with God operating in them. Through the living of community life that they had experienced with the Master, an order began to emerge. John brings out beautifully in his Gospel how the Lord intended His community to have shepherds to guide and protect it (John 21). The invisible guidance and protection of the Spirit, preservation from evil, and sanctification (John 17.11-19) do not exclude earthly direction. It is precisely in the very spiritual Gospel of John that we sense an insistence on the Church as a visible society existing in the world, though one that transcends the world (John 17.15ff.).

The early Christians saw themselves as the communities of believers guided by the disciples, living a life of true fraternal charity, and growing daily through their study of the Word and celebration of the Eucharist. Newcomers became united to the Church through Baptism. Eucharist and Baptism were much more than mere external remembrances or rites. There was no well-defined theology of the Sacraments to confuse people with abstract explanations, but realization of the true meaning of these sacred signs, through which the power of the Risen Lord was communicated to them.

Development of the Church

The Church has gone through various periods of development. It has had its share of good times and more than its share of bad times. One is tempted to ask, if this is the Church of Jesus Christ and if it is guided and protected by the Spirit, why is it beset with trouble and scandal? If the Church is divine, why isn't it perfect?

We tend to forget that the Church is a living, growing body. The Father sent His Son on a mission to begin the task of uniting the world to Himself. Christ came to win hearts so that, through faith in the way of the Lord, people could freely unite themselves to Him and begin the new creation. God does not suspend the forces of human development at work in His world. We know that the development of a child follows certain lines, and we also know through anthropology that the growth of cultures also follows certain slow processes of change. If we keep in mind that the Church is a living body, we may be able to understand the different stages of the Church's development by comparing it to the development of a person.

Psychologists are discovering how important the first six years of a child's life are for the proper development of his personality. During these years, there is a very rapid physical and mental growth. The newborn, while enjoying the milk of his mother's breast, begins to learn the joy of giving to fulfill the needs of another. The infant sees the joy in the mother's smile as she nourishes him; he feels the warmth and comfort of her arms. In an obscure way he experiences from the beginning the joy that is associated with giving. The more the child experiences joy in giving, the more he will learn that there is joy in being with others, and especially in giving oneself to others.

This was the experience of the early Church that witnessed the tender, loving care of its Founder. The early Church knew who it was and where it was going. During the first six hundred years the Church grew in numbers and communities. Its personality was formed, but the next few hundred years, as in the development of an individual, were painful and confusing.

Young children have very active imaginations; they are interested in tales and are fond of superman stories. So it was with the young Church. People became very interested in the great wonders and miracles of the past and tales about the saints. Stories of superhuman powers of the saints were quick to circulate. The religiosity of the early Church was the natural religiosity of the child. The liturgical life of the Church was understood by many as magical rites and rituals performed by the clergy. The people stood at a distance and watched, with varying degrees of interest and awe, the beautiful sacred plays.

As young children are fond of building forts and castles, so the early Church became very concerned with buildings. The age of the great cathedrals, monasteries and basilicas appeared. Like young children, the early Church was prone to associate with bad friends. What happens so often to children in bad company frequently happened to the Church too. In many things, it took on the ways of the princes of the world rather than guiding the world to take the ways of the Prince of Peace.

Yet the most difficult period was still ahead — the important years of adolescence. With adolescence came the break with the world of childhood, self-assertion, the discovery of reason, and the lean towards rationalism. But God, as the perfect Father, did not enslave His growing Church; He would not keep it from maturing. God respected His growing child and allowed it to follow Scholasticism, Rationalism, and Positivism. The youngster was not sure of itself; it was wavering, striving for self-identity. The youngster became proud, self-centered, and self-assured, almost to the point of destroying itself.

Nevertheless, at the very time when nearsighted prophets of doom were proclaiming the death of the Church, the maturing community of believers moved towards a new plateau. A traumatic moment of self-discovery arrived. The phenomenon of Vatican II manifested, in a sense, the Church's coming of age. Some pastoral theologians have stated that after the first six hundred years of life, the Church stopped proclaiming and started defending itself. The 7th century to the 20th century was, in some respects, like a great parenthesis. This defensive attitude did not come to an end until Vatican II. (See Alfonso Nebreda, *Kerygma in Crisis*.)

I would like to go even further and see the Church as the prodigal son of Luke's Gospel. In his surge for self-discovery and self-assertion, he went to other lands, as the Church went off to seek understanding of itself in the various philosophies of the day. During the period of adolescence, the Church became extremely interested in itself, seeking to discover and define itself. Yet with Vatican II, the Church returned to the house of the Father. It rediscovered its mission of service not only to the sons and daughters but to all the world. The Church rediscovered that, like the Master, it is to work not for itself but for others, and that love means giving to another. It is no wonder that the masterpiece of the Council is the "Pastoral Constitution on the Church in the Modern World." The child has come of age; it has matured into an adult. The Church is now prepared to take its place of leadership in the integral development of humanity and the world.

Far from scandalizing us, the history of the Church should lead us to an even deeper faith and appreciation of the ways of God with man. God does not destroy the ways of man in order to perfect him. God accepts man as he is and where he is. The good father of a mature and successful young man who has come through all the healthy troubles and tribulations of normal growth can point to his son with pride and

113

say: "You would never believe all the trouble that kid of ours got into during his school days." Perhaps God today sees the world in the same manner, as the mature child of his tender, loving, and patient care, the Church come of age.

Emergence of the New Creation

"The Church believes that Christ, who died and was raised up for all, can through His Spirit offer man the light and the strength to measure up to his supreme destiny. . . . She likewise holds that in her most benign Lord and Master can be found the key, the focal point, and the goal of all human history. . . . Hence in the light of Christ, the image of the unseen God, the firstborn of every creature, the Council wishes to speak to all men in order to illuminate the mystery of man and to cooperate in finding the solution to the outstanding problems of our time."[2]

As the continuation of the Risen Lord in time and space, the Church sees its presence in the world as one directed to service. To serve and not be served is the solitary goal of the Church. According to Vatican II, the Church must serve the world by seeking to read and scrutinize the signs of the times, by guiding man through the crises of rapid change, not only giving meaning to progress, but initiating and stimulating even new kinds of progress presently unforseen by humanity. Nothing that is genuinely human can fail to raise an echo in the hearts of the faithful. Faith throws a new light on everything, manifests God's design for man's total vocation, and directs the mind to solutions that are fully human.[3]

The Church has come to a more mature awareness of its duty to further the growth of mankind. As Christ penetrated the whole of creation, so now the Church through a service of creative love must penetrate every corner of the vast cosmos.

Today, man has become his own self-creator to a degree previously undreamed of. Man is probing space and, through the discoveries of RNA and DNA, probing the mystery of his own existence. Increasingly, modern man will not be the product of fate, but the product of what he fashions. Man is taking God seriously by taking the world seriously. He is accepting the challenge to become God's partner in the evolution of the world. As is evident from the "Pastoral Constitution of the Church in the Modern World," the Church is no longer running away from this world; it is not frightened by advances in science, technology, and the arts.

The Church's mission does not originate in science, education, or technology. Yet, it must seek to penetrate and bring to perfection every aspect of man and his creation by living out and proclaiming the Master's message of love. The Church seeks to bind up the wounds of the sick and to feed the mouths of the hungry, but this is only part of its mission. It must stand as a clear witness in today's world and proclaim that progress is not genuine if universal, personalizing love is missing. Love is the one and only psycho-physical energy capable of bringing about the integral development of the world and the true liberation of persons and nations.

The Church and human progress are not to be identified with each other, but neither can they be seen independently of each other. As the phylum of love operating within the phylum of man, the Church is the axis upon which the evolution of the world is progressing. The Christian holds the key to the natural movement of evolution, since Christian charity is the natural movement towards fulfillment in Christ, the final stage or Omega point of Teilhard. This charity provides a force for the unification of man that is far stronger than anything in evolution. Christian charity urges us from within to build a better world here on earth and to be in the very first ranks of every campaign for the authentic and integral progress of mankind.

From the New, a New Creature Develops

The Church does not exist apart from its members as our bodies do not exist apart from our cells. The cells, in organic union with one another, make up the body. It is their individuality and mutual interdependence that enables the body to be a well-organized unit. To the degree that the cells are healthy and working together, the body functions properly; as the cells become sick and degenerate, the body weakens and eventually dies. So it is with the Church. Each member must be spiritually alive, healthy, and full of life-energy if the Church is to live its mission to the world. The Church is not just the pope, bishops, and priests, but all Christians together in the fellowship of life, charity, and truth.[4]

As the Church is not a finished product, but a growing organism that goes through the stages of maturation, the same is true with each Christian. Each person must make his own journey to a visible and concrete entry into the community through Baptism. He must seek the way to mature Christian life, and ultimately to the glorious moment of final decision at the instant of death.

The community is the source of our Christian personhood. Our experience of interpersonal encounter within the believing community opens into a similar, though infinitely more mysterious, relationship of duality in unity. This is the supreme I-Thou relationship with the humanity of Jesus, the

116

sacrament of God and our personal contact with transcendence. This relationship enables me to go beyond my physical limitations into the realm of true fulfillment. It is in the life of fellowship with the believing community that the Risen Lord continues to exist. Christian faith, which occurs through personal encounter with the Risen Lord, appears only in community experience.

It is precisely at this point of conversion that our true selves comes forth with such force that we are new creatures. God, who knows us with all our defects, has accepted us for what we are and loves us without reservation. We experience great joy for being loved simply for what we are! Even more, God not only accepts us and loves us, He forgives us. When we experience forgiveness, we experience most deeply the transforming power of love.

We cannot love when the feeling of rejection nags us, even if the rejection is justified. Enmity exists towards our neighbor when we feel he condemns us, even if such a condemnation is not expressed in words. As long as we feel rejected by God, we cannot love Him, and we strive not to know Him. This is the deepest source of existential anxiety; to not be accepted by God is to be rejected by Him. Everything changes when we experience God calling us into fellowship with Him. This is a radical change that seizes the whole of our human existence: our relationship to God, to ourselves, with our fellowmen, and with the whole world.

This experience of a forgiving God is the basis of true love of neighbor. God loves me in spite of my actions. No matter how unlovable, lowly, and ugly I may think of myself, God loves me in a deeply personal way. Regardless of what I may think of myself, God sees something lovable in me. Because

God has accepted me as I am, however bad my past might have been (see John 4.10; 15.12; Romans 8.31; Galatians 2.20), I can and must love my neighbor, forgive him, accept him as he is. The experience of God loving me helps me to surmount the natural barriers of loving even the apparently unlovable person. This is the love that creates a mature person. This love is the core of each Christian community and the axis for the whole body of communities. It is the psycho-physical energy that makes possible the true progress of the world.

What does it mean for me to be a Christian? I discover that people are better looking than before because I see them with new eyes. I discover that conversation is richer and infinitely more interesting because I listen with new ears. I no longer have to hide my real self because others know me as I am. Life is no longer a riddle, a series of seeming contradictions or chance happenings. It is the joy of living for others and knowing that even in failure we are important enough to be loved. Life is not a lonely trail into the unknown, but a group pilgrimage struggling in joy and sorrow towards the Father's house. Life is no longer a slavery to fate, but the freedom to be myself in cooperation with others. It is the patience to accept what cannot be changed, the sense of urgency and courage to improve what can be improved, and the wisdom to discern one from the other. Being a Christian means living life to the fullest.

I first experience this love of God from my parents, later in the fellowship of a struggling Christian community. This lived experience takes on definite meaning for me through the study of the Word, as interpreted through the living Church. Through the daily struggle of Christian living, and nourished by the Eucharistic Celebration, I have experienced the warm, creating love of God that enables me to destroy selfishness and my fake self. Christian love has not inhibited the human love in me; it has deepened it. Christian love has allowed my true self to come forth; it has enabled me to become a new creature.

The Meaning of Christogenesis

Many today claim that Christianity will not work. Christianity has not been tried and found wanting; it has been found difficult and therefore not tried. When it has been tried, Christianity has produced authentic lovers of mankind, who in a radiant freedom from self-concern, have revealed the breadth of experience into which the human spirit can move. These have been men who have died to themselves and have lived, who have forgotten themselves and have found their true selves, who have enjoyed the fullness of human joy in Christian living.

It has been said that modern civilization could not have been built upon the foundation of the words of Jesus. That may be true. It is also true that what could be built upon His words would be something much better than our modern civilization.

By a curious contrast, practical men today are finding their thoughts drawn again to the impractical Jesus. Has much of our carefully organized and ordered life been moving in the wrong direction? Is the acquisition of money, property, cars, clothes, and recreation the goal of life? Or is there something more that is needed to bring authentic peace and joy into the lives of men and nations? Man must develop his own potential and the potential of his world to the full, but will the material pursuits alone ever suffice for true happiness?

119

The answer to this question, to the mystery of what man is, lies in the mystery of the person of Jesus. Only in the mystery of the Incarnate Word does the mystery of man receive light. Christ fully reveals man to man himself and makes his supreme calling clear.[5] The unfolding of Christ in the world becomes the unfolding of mankind's capacity to evolve — God's free gift to men in Christ.

Part Three

The
Divine-Human
Adventure

chapter seven

The Mystery of
Suffering in Christ

To Face or to Avoid the Issue

We are accustomed to saying that life is a vale of tears. Today the saying is no longer fashionable. People want to live with the pretence that everything is just fine. We learn to put on the proper face for school, work, church, or the club. We are hypnotized with the illusion that modern science has answers for all our problems. If we are physically ill, we are confident that an injection or operation will restore us to health. The middle-aged are confident that the health club will restore the slim lines of youth. If our skin is beginning to show its age, Max Factor has the right cosmetic to bring back the fresh look. For those beginning to feel that everyone is crazy, there is a psychologist around to restore the proper balance. If we feel depressed or rejected, a round of golf or perhaps a vacation will do the trick.

On we go, even to the point of attempting to remove death from the field of our experience.[1] We seek to escape from words that express the end: death, corpse, funeral, etc. We attempt to run away from the reality that no person can escape: death.

The more we study the world the more we discover that everything has a purpose. An answer to the mystery of man's existence cannot be found apart from the mystery of suffering and death. The mystery of suffering has plagued men's minds for at least as long as recorded history. In spite of all the advances of modern civilization, why do people still suffer? Man has progressed a long way, yet there are still people plagued with incurable cancer, leprosy, deformity, mental illness, and insanity. There are still hunger, social oppression, economic slavery, war, illiteracy. Why?

What Man Has Made of Man

We are ready to admit that much of the suffering in the world today is caused by the selfishness, egotism, laziness, and destructiveness of men. The victims of gang beatings, stabbings and shootings, incapacitation from war, and the mental breakdown of the wife of an alcoholic husband are but a few examples of modern suffering. The sin of each person contributes to the destruction and breakdown of another person.

There is still another aspect to the mystery of suffering. In an earlier chapter, we alluded to man's refusal to take himself and the world seriously. For too long, we have wanted to sit on the sidelines, like the pagan gods of old who laughed and played while the world suffered. Only in recent times have men started to take their role as co-creators seriously. Earnest efforts have been made to eliminate hunger by developing better crops and cattle, to stamp out illiteracy by providing better schooling even in the remote areas of the world, to improve health by better surgical procedures and medicines.

In spite of all this, we are still moving too slowly. Progress is not dictated by love and interest for the human family but simply by a search for products that will bring larger profits. Time, money, and talent are wasted on weapons of war and destruction. Man still seeks to destroy man on a far greater scale than ever before. Suffering is again an effect of man's sin and failure.

We see the Christian as the true light of the world. He is one who not only stands for progress in medicine, technology, the arts, education, and government, but for the evolution of the world towards perfection. He is the realist who can see the world for what it really is.

What is the role of suffering in all this? Suffering is a part of life. We cannot escape it. As long as there is misery in the world, man still has a job to do in perfecting the universe. Suffering becomes a light upon the mountaintop, reminding man that he still has a long way to go. As pain in my body is a signal to me that something is wrong, so any type of human suffering is a signal that humanity is still imperfect, that something is wrong that has to be put right. We hardly need the message of Christ to see in suffering a blunt indication that mankind has not yet achieved perfection.

Have you ever visited people in tuberculosis wards? Have you ever been with a terminal cancer patient who has developed an immunity to all drugs, suffers painful bedsores, and prays for death? Have you ever seen a leper whose hands are missing? Have you ever felt helplessness before a deformed child? Have you ever stood by the deathbed of a beautiful young girl dying of leukemia? Have you ever been face-to-face with such misery and human suffering that you instinctively ask; "My God, how can you allow this?" Some ask, if there is a God, how can He be so cruel? Yet the real question should be, why has man done so little?

Bishop Fulton Sheen once said that the great tragedy was not that there was so much suffering in the world, but that so much suffering was wasted because it had no meaning. Teilhard saw suffering among the great mysteries. To me, suffering is incomprehensible and absurd without the light of God's redeeming and recreating love. Without the message of the Cross-Resurrection, suffering and death are absurd.

Love and Suffering

Throughout these reflections we have tried to show that Christianity, far from attempting to escape the world, loves the world. Our God became fully flesh; He immersed Himself completely in this world to lead the world to perfection. We need only to "put on" Him.

The Christian must love the world, but he must transcend the world. He must go beyond the limits of the material world. Man's constant temptation is to close himself in rather than to open himself to the beyond.

It seems to be a contradiction that God who so loved the world as to give His only begotten Son would then tell man through His Son: "Whoever wishes to be my follower must deny his very self, take up his cross each day, and follow in my steps." (Luke 9.23) But there is no contradiction. To love is to suffer. Love forces us to be open. Because of selfishness, we are prone to turn in to ourselves rather than open to others. This opening of oneself and going beyond oneself to the other is a painful process.

The Son came on a mission to initiate us into the fullness of life, which is the happiness of loving. Christ revealed this to us through every word and action. This is the meaning of the Christ-event; when the Word became flesh, love became suffering. In God, love is the happiness of a complete, mutual gift; in man, love is the renunciation of self-love.

This is far easier understood than achieved. We are tied to ourselves. We like being selfish. It is enjoyable to think of myself first. Because the world is what it is, there is no way to love without suffering, without having to accept disappointment.

To love is to be vulnerable, for the person whom I love will not necessarily love me. My beloved can cause me sleepless nights, make suffering my lot. Yet love does not cease if it is really love. The unwillingness to accept this risk is the agony of hell, the only place where one is safe from love.

Yet, in this painful emptying of oneself, a new being is born that does not exist by itself, but in relationship to the other. In loving, I allow my new self to break forth. The more I love, the more I will surrender myself into the hands of my beloved. Love involves the risk of surrendering myself to another person whose freedom and loyalty can threaten me and through whose life suffering can enter mine.

Love involves an opening of oneself, a breaking of the bonds of selfishness, self-sufficiency, and pride. It is an opening of oneself to allow another to become part of me. Love springs from a humble admission that I cannot live alone, that I need help. Love is not merely giving; it is also receiving, allowing another the joy of giving to me.

I remember an uncle who was a country doctor in an impoverished area of Mexico. He used to tell me how important it was to sit at the table with even the poorest of the poor and share their meal. He said, "If I refuse I insult them. My refusal will be interpreted to mean that I don't need them." My uncle never became rich, but he was a happy person. He enjoyed travelling on horseback across the hot desert plains to minister to his patients and he allowed them the joy of ministering to him. From him, I learned an important lesson: never refuse the gift of a poor person; accepting it, you accept him. You give him the joy and satisfaction of being able to give you something.

As I have tried to bring out, it is through truly meaningful personal relations with others that I enter into the supreme I-Thou relationship between God and myself. But the horizontal alone would finish in a dead end, or even worse, could become a long road leading to nowhere. It is through the horizontal that I must come to the vertical relationship between God and myself. In this vertical relationship, I am enabled to reenter human relationships in a more intense way.

To Believe is to Play for Keeps

When a person says, "Lord, I believe!", more than his intellect is involved. Faith is an act of the whole person. This is true even on the purely human level. The more I know and love you the more my whole self will be ready to trust you even in the face of contradictory evidence. The mother who discovers her son is a criminal would still rather believe him rather than the others, in spite of the most convincing evidence against him. A girl who falls in love with a boy regarded as worthless by others would also rather believe him than the others.

Is this to say that love, faith, and trust are irrational? No, it is merely reaffirming that personal faith, which leads to love, and which, in turn, engenders trust, involves the whole personality. Faith is an act in which both the rational and the nonrational elements of the person are transcended. On the other hand, faith is not merely an emotional experience. Belief encompasses the whole person — intellect, will, emotions, and passions, all working in harmony with each other in opening the whole person fully to belief.

Examine your personal relationships with those whom you truly love. What do you really mean when you say, "I believe you?" The more we realize what it takes to believe, the more we discover that it requires courage even to begin to surrender ourselves in belief. This opening of the self to others involves great risk and many uncertainties, and the possibility of failure. Yet, if a man wants really to live, he must take the risk. The risk makes life worth living. In every human relationship there is the possibility of failure and the risk of suffering frustration for having surrendered oneself to someone who was unworthy of it. There is even the possibility of total despair.

In genuine relationships, there will be a certain degree of surrender to the other. Only in the relationship between God and myself can this surrender be unconditional. This is not to say that there will no longer be any doubts. The possibility that I could be wrong is really a confirmation of faith. Doubt means that I take this new relationship seriously enough to be concerned about it.

God has taken me seriously enough to accept me for what I am, to forgive me, and to love me. He invites me to do the same, to take Him seriously and to work with Him in the world to my fullest capacity. I must do whatever I can to improve this world. The Christian is one who loves the world, yet transcends the world. He loves what is, but he loves even more what is yet to be. This is re-creation of the world in Christ.

Christian Witness

Jesus tells us to take up our crosses and follow Him, but He does not tell us to look for crosses. We are to take them willingly in whatever form they may come. Through faith we surrender ourselves totally to the will of the Father. Prepared to do all we can for the sickness of the world, we must be ready to accept that our best is not always sufficient. With the Lord at the Mount of Olives, we pray: "Father, if it is your will, take this cup from me; yet not my will but yours be done." (Luke 22.42)

At these moments of supreme suffering, the Christian becomes a sign to those around him. He accepts his suffering, not because he enjoys it, but because he has faith in the way of the Father, a way that is often incomprehensible to man.

Suffering brings us face-to-face with our limitations and imperfections. If life is to have meaning, we must look beyond the here-and-now. The inner joy of the person in great pain fulfills to the highest degree the Christian vocation of giving to others. His very suffering becomes a radiant light. He tells the world around him how much more there is to life than merely material things.

Suffering is a reminder that we are not made for this world, that we are not of this sin-world and that the sin-world must be converted. C.S. Lewis says that suffering "plants the flag of truth within the fortress of a rebel soul." The Christian who has accepted his cross is a blazing symbol to the world, showing that, through the living way of the cross, through surrender to the will of the Father, we pass to the fullness of life.

An Ursuline sister working in Bangkok told me about a young Buddhist who wanted to join the religion class. When asked her reason, the student answered: "My Catholic friend radiates a love and joy that I cannot explain. I believe her faith as a Christian is the root of this; I want to have a share in this love and joy, too."

The sister knew the reason for the Catholic girl's inner joy. The girl had suffered much in her life. Both her mother and father had given up their religion; her eldest sister had married a Buddhist; her uncle was the "Al Capone" of Bangkok. This young girl had endured much humiliation from gossip about her family. As a result she showed a rare sensitivity towards her companions.

She had discovered in Christ a way of giving every moment of the day to her friends. She would always listen, and would gracefully sacrifice herself for others. She had a deep spirit of prayer. This sensitivity that she had developed through her own suffering became the light for others to discover a richer way of life.

Intimate Participation in Christ's Suffering

Pain and suffering are signs that the world has a long way to go on the road toward perfection. Acceptance of necessary suffering is a sign of our confidence and surrender to the Divine Will. Is suffering something more yet?

"Even now I find my joy in the suffering I endure for you. In my own flesh I fill up what is lacking in the sufferings of Christ for the sake of his body, the Church." (Colossians 1.24) Christ suffered not because He loved suffering; He feared it as we do. But He loves us, and to love is to suffer. Christ suffered not because of sin, for He was sinless, but because of the sins of others. Wisdom and free choice dictated crucifixion of the flesh so that the spirit might be freed.

131

"It was for this you were called, since Christ suffered for you in just this way and left you an example, to have you follow in his footsteps." (1 Peter 2.21) For us today, suffering is sacred because it confers the most intimate resemblance to the Son whose passion and cross saved the world. There is nothing that brings people closer than fighting for a common cause. All this suffering together builds up a special bond of unity, unintelligible to one who has not experienced it. The bond of unity we have with the Lord, who invites us to join Him in redeeming the world is even more incomprehensible. Through our suffering we are invited to offer ourselves in a most personal union with Christ. To say yes to this invitation is to enter into a more intense realm of love. Suffering and acceptance become the outward signs of a love that entrusts us entirely to Christ.

As Christ did not seek the cross, I am not to seek crosses. But I should encounter my crosses with the prayer that I may have the strength to accept them. I pray also that I may be able to suffer, not only because I have sinned, but because Christ, who suffered, has invited me into intimate union with Him. Through my firm belief in the solidarity of the human family, I am able to see my sufferings as a means to salvation for others. Christ suffered for me, so I pray that I may be united with Him in His suffering for our fellowmen.

Anticipation of Evolution

There is another characteristic of suffering in an evolving world. The whole cosmos has gradually been unfolding in the direction of life. Life evolves towards consciousness, and consciousness in man transforms itself into spirit, the capacity of being in union with others and eventually with the absolute.

If I analyze my interpersonal relations, I discover that, though they usually begin with the physical and the sensible, I reach a point of intensity in which my physical body, rather than helping, seems to prevent me from totally giving and receiving. Man himself is a microcosmos who goes through the various stages of evolution and, at a certain time in his life, may surpass, or anticipate, the present state of evolution in the world.

"Suffering is still to be treated at first as an adversary and fought against right to the end; yet at the same time, we must accept it insofar as it can uproot our egoism and center us more completely in God. Yes, dark and repulsive though it is, suffering has been revealed to us as a supremely active principle for the humanization and divinization of the universe. Here is the ultimate meaning of the cross . . . a growth of spirit arising from the deficiency of matter, . . . a possible Christification of suffering. This is indeed the miracle which has been constantly renewed for the last two thousand years."[2]

As evolution is an ascent towards consciousness, so the growth of each person is an ascent towards the fullness of personality. Personalization comes not through isolation, but through union. It is a union that does not crush the parts, but one that respects differences. The more "other" one is in a union, the more he discovers himself. Such a personalizing union cannot occur without love, for love alone is capable of uniting in a way that completes and fulfills the parts.

Union with another requires a partial dying. Union in love is a foretaste of the "leap out of ourselves which must in the end deliver us from the bondage of ourselves into the service of the divine sovereignty."[3] This spiritualization of our desires and aspirations develops our personality to its highest intensity. A crisis accepted and surmounted reveals to us that we are now, in reality, freer and more active.

Through suffering that is accepted, material deficiencies and limitations take a secondary role. Consciousness is liberated, allowing us to come to an ever more perfect union with the Supreme Consciousness, so that the individual reflects what the universe will be at the end of time. The evolving of consciousness is an evolving towards spiritualization, not in the sense of spirit as opposed to matter, but spirit as the creative life of love. Just as psychic torture is more effective than physical torture, so suffering that is freely accepted, or spiritualized, purifies one more deeply of egotism and selfishness. By freely accepting suffering, the true self is allowed to emerge and enter into a more perfect union with the Godhead. A person anticipates the evolution of the world by uniting himself freely, or spiritually, with the Divine.

There are two examples in my own life that may clarify the point. As a young seminarian, I visited the mother of a large family in the hospital. She had had a serious operation, her husband had been suffering from tuberculosis, and things on the farm were anything but good. I can still remember clearly her beautiful smile when she told me, "I cannot understand why God loves me so very much. He is allowing me to share in the saving sufferings of His Son."

I have visited this woman several times since then. Her family always had more than its share of troubles, yet I have never heard her complain. The inner joy and peace that radiates from her is one of the best sermons I have ever heard on suffering. Such people are not escaping from life, but have learned to take life seriously. When suffering comes into their lives, they genuinely accept it as a sign of God's special blessing, for they realize that their suffering has drawn them closer to Christ.

The second example concerns my father, and was probably the most formative element in my life. Things were never easy for him. At a very early age he had to leave home to seek employment in the United States to support the family. He took life seriously and worked to the best of his ability. He was a man of prayer, but prayer in him was never a substitute for work or human ingenuity. There was always sacrifice, yet he was the happiest man I have ever known. He worked hard to give us, his family, what he himself had never been able to enjoy. Only now do I fully appreciate the reason for his happiness. His whole life was a giving of himself, so that others might have what he did not have, and not have to suffer what he suffered.

But the strongest lesson came in the last days of my father's life, before he died of cancer. He had been fighting it for several years, but it finally conquered him. His last few weeks were spent in great agony, yet never once did I hear him complain. His only prayer was one of constant thanksgiving; he was so grateful because God had given him much more than he had ever asked for. Towards the end, in spite of his agony, he realized that it was Halloween night. The children would be out trick-or-treating. He had mother call the store to send over a large sack of candy for the nurses to take home to their children. He lived in order to give, and, even in dying, he sought to give.

To me, my father gave not only life, but a powerful example of how true joy is living for others. To me, my father is the life example of what I have been laboriously trying to say in these pages.

chapter eight

The Mystery of Death in Christ

No Man Can Speak From Experience

The greatest human mystery is death. No one has ever returned to tell us what happens in death. We have seen people die; we have read about death, and we have been to funerals and cemeteries. I feel great sorrow when someone dies whom I love very dearly. However, this does not necessarily help me to face the real question, the one that I cannot escape whether I want to or not. What will happen when I die?

When we are born, there is only one thing certain for our future. Someday we will die. Aside from that, people cannot, on their own, find a truly satisfactory explanation to the meaning of death.

We live in an age that prides itself on a realistic approach to life, and yet the most evident and certain reality is passed over in silence. I can pretend to ignore death, but in reality I only succeed in making my existence unauthentic; my life will be lessened by evasion of the key issue. If you do not want to think about death, think of its alternative — a long drawn-out senility. If this were the ultimate reality, I would have to agree with Sartre and Camus that life is nonsense.

Man is not powerless against death. Man can and does overcome death by finding God in it. Christ has conquered death, not by suppressing it, but by reversing its effect. In the Christian message, we discover the formula for happiness in life and the meaning of physical death. We become aware of death's role in the gradual evolution of a person from birth towards the fulfillment of his being.

Final Decision

If we think about our own life, we will discover a very complex drama. Instinctively we know that we are free, yet the more we analyze our actions, the more we realize how little freedom we actually have. We are conditioned by our parents, family, teachers, friends, neighborhood, church, club, what we read, the movies, and television. Outside influences can be so great that some people claim we are never really free.

Yet there will be a moment in my life when I will be totally free. There will be no one around to influence me, to aid me, or to restrain me. The doctors, the nurses, my closest friends might all be standing around, but they will be powerless. For the first time in my life I will be totally alone. I will no longer even be able to cry for help. People and things dear to me in life will cease to exist. For the first time in my life, I will be my true self. It is death that provides the entrance into my inmost self.[1]

At the instant of death, all the masks I have worn will fall off; all the roles I have played will come to an end; all my running away will cease. The people who have dominated me will be gone; the crutches I have used through life will crumble and disappear. Everything that has kept me from seeing my true self and my God will be gone. The fully mature and perfect me will be born, free. Death is birth, the entry into the unceasing, intensively lived present.

I will enter into a fascinating and terrifying adventure. For the first time in my life I will be perfectly free. I will also enter into the presence of the Lord of Creation. I will be face-to-face with Christ, in complete freedom and with the utmost clarity of mind. At the instant of death, I will be faced with my final decision. This decision is not made during the final agony, nor does it come after death; it is precisely at the moment of death when I cross the threshold of time and space into the unceasing, cosmic *Now*. At this moment I finalize my life for eternity. Death is existential fulfillment beyond time and space. Becoming ends where Being begins. "Only in death, therefore, does man reach the total unity of his being; he gets away from the universal constriction and unease and enters into the depths of the world, into the 'heart of the universe.' "[2]

Our life is a preparation for entry into the fullness of life. The moment of meeting Christ face-to-face should not be feared by one who has been striving to live. The person who, through his actions, has been coming closer to the God of love, has nothing to fear (Matthew 25.31-46). We will die as we live. Death will be a consummation of everything we have been working for throughout life. We shall then *be* what we have been *becoming*.

Every man has kept a certain distance from God during life. At death, that distance will be no more. We meet the radiant, loving Christ calling us to Himself. To accept His invitation is to enter the fullness of joy, peace, and happiness. To refuse is to burn eternally in the great love that has been experienced and freely rejected. It is the fire burning within us when we, through our own fault, lose something that could have been ours. If we accept Christ's invitation, we are totally united in the unending ecstasy of perfect love, given and received.

The outcome of this final decision will depend on us. What we want to be in the future, we must begin to be in the present. It is the individual, seemingly insignificant decisions of everyday living that prepare us for the great and final decision at the moment of death. God is constantly inviting; the way we respond disposes and conditions us for the final response.

When we pass through the gateway of death the new life of the universal cosmic presence, we are beyond the limits of time and space. Because we never manage to be free from time and space in this life, it is impossible for us to understand what happens at death.

The Purifying Fire of Love

To encounter the risen Lord, person-to-person, in the fire of His love for me is at once the supreme fulfillment and the most terrible suffering. The fulfillment comes in the measure that I have responded to His love; the suffering comes to the degree I have rejected His love out of my selfishness, egotism, pride, and laziness. The nakedness that Adam and Eve experienced when they were face-to-face with God parallels the guilt within me when I am face-to-face with the One whom I know I have offended. The more I have offended Him, the more I will feel the pains of my guilt. The love of God breaks through to the inmost core of my being, burning away the remaining layers of selfishness and sin. The more dirt and trash I have accumulated, the more intense the pain of the purifying love of God will be. The intensity of the purification needed could be compared to the accumulated suffering of one's entire life. In reality it is the suffering of a lifetime concentrated into an instant.

Fire purifies gold. A person who has allowed himself to get out of shape physically must diet and sweat away the calories in order to become what he ought to be. The worse the condition is, the more rigorous the diet and the exercise will have to be. Because man loves his health, he is willing to go through the necessary purification. So it is with life. Throughout life we allow ourselves to accumulate various fat layers: egotism, selfishness, cruelty to others, laziness, self-righteousness, etc. These have to be destroyed so that the image and likeness of God in us can come forth. Only then can I enter into the most perfect love affair possible. Through the cosmic Christ, and in union with Him, I share a unity with my parents, friends, relatives, mankind, and the world.

Should we cease praying for the dead or the dying? Not at all! From the earliest times, Christians have intuitively prayed for the dying and the dead. This intuition is a genuine expression of faith. We are one body, and in the same body, other cells come to the rescue of the cell in distress. This is what we do by our prayers. The Father has told us to ask, and we will receive. Our prayers, uttered in time and space, help the person in need at the instant of death, though it is the borderland of time and space. Though totally alone at the moment of death, we are not beyond the aid of our fellow Christians.

We believe in the communion of saints; we are united with and aided by their prayers and good works, by those still on earth, by those now passing through the moment of death, and by those already in the fullness of life.

Let us remember that for God, all is present. For Him, our prayer for a dead person and the actual death of that person coincide. For him the human being, whom we love and whose decision we want to make easier by the support of our prayer, is dying at the moment when we are praying for him. Our intercession can never arrive too late, even if we are praying for him decades after his death. "At every moment of our life, we can sustain in him the greatest decision of his life."[3]

The Meaning of Christian Resignation

Many have criticized Christianity as being a religion of the hereafter. This to a degree is true, but, like many partial truths, it can be more dangerous than a lie. Christianity is not only faith in the hereafter, but faith in the here-and-now. Of all the religions known to man, there is no other that calls for love of this world as much. Yet through a false understanding of Christian resignation, many have preached only part of the message. It became the gospel of suffering and sacrifice here on earth, so that you could enjoy the happiness of heaven after death. If we disdain human progress and development, Christianity becomes a "pie in the sky."

Thanks to God, Vatican II has rejected this heresy of the love of suffering for the sake of suffering. The "Pastoral Constitution of the Church in the Modern World" is a clear presentation of the essence of the Christian message: take the totality of man and his world seriously. Christianity is concerned for the whole man: his birth, his life, and his death. The improvement and development of the whole man is the mission of Christ. "I came that they might have life and have it to the full." (John 10.10) "A false interpretation of Christian resignation, together with a false idea of Christian detachment, is

141

the principal source of the antagonisms which make a great many Gentiles so sincerely hate the Gospel."[4]

The Christian must be able to distinguish two great aspects of Christian living. The first is a sincere effort to improve the quality of life for himself and for those around him, to struggle against the evils of hunger, substandard education, poor housing, unjust wages, crime, and even death. Because he loves the world, and because the Father loves the world, he gives all that he is and all that he has to the development of the world. The second aspect of Christian living asks that the Christian must be ready to face defeat, and to achieve victory in the transfiguration of defeat.

When the Gospel is properly presented, it condemns those who disregard the earth and foster passivity in the face of evil. Cultivation of suffering and diminishment as values in themselves perverts the Christian Gospel. False detachment is an enemy of Christianity, a most dangerous type of wolf in sheep's clothing. Such perverted Christianity has slowed the conversion of the world. "A religion which is judged to be inferior to our human ideal . . . is already *condemned*. It is therefore of supreme importance for the Christian to understand and live submission to the will of God in an *active* sense which, as we have said, is the only orthodox sense."[5]

Through our faith, we can see the world and mankind as they really are. Their true dignity becomes apparent. We are armed with the firm hope that our contribution, however small and insignificant it may seem, will contribute to the building of the ultimate earth, the Parousia. Yet, in all human successes and failures, the Christian recognizes in faith a further dimension, suprasensible transformation and growth. The resignation of a Christian is not a psychological escape from reality. It is a trust that lifts the field of his activity above the zone of sensible reality. When evil comes, he is not defeated, but he joins in perfect communion with God to transform evil into good.

Christian renunciation must always satisfy two conditions: it must enable us to go beyond everything in the world; and at the same time it must compel us to press forward with conviction for the development of this world. "Give me the strength to change what has to be changed, the courage to accept what cannot be changed, and the wisdom to distinguish the two."

chapter nine

The Mystery of Human Fulfillment in Christ

Human Life and Death

In these reflections we have attempted to emphasize Christianity as a faith for the here-and-now. Through his faith, man enters into the community of mankind with a new vigor and dedication to authentic progress. Yet when the temporal here-and-now comes to an end, the eternal, ever-present *Now* begins. Christianity, as preached by the Master, offers a new life, beginning here on earth, and perfected beyond the limits of time and space.

The constant message of Scripture is that human life is biological, but much more than merely biological. Man is a creature made to the image and likeness of God. Man is the glory of God. He is fully alive when he lives the life of the Spirit and the life of goodness. In so doing, he is united with God. We are alive to the degree that we are united with God. Similarly, the real death of man is not biological death, but the death of his egotism, selfishness, and laziness that have separated him from God. When man lives the life of evil, or as Scripture calls it, the life of the flesh, he is separated from God and is dead. Through sin, man experiences a death that

144

goes beyond mere biological death. In man, the death of the flesh and all that is evil, is the birth of the life of the Spirit. It is only through the Spirit that we begin to live the authentic human life.

The true Christian has already died and is now living the life of the Risen Lord. "Are you not aware that we who were baptized into Christ Jesus were baptized into His death? Through baptism in His death we were buried with Him, so . . . we too might live with new life. . . . This we know: our old self was crucified with him so that the sinful body might be destroyed. . . . In the same way, you must consider yourselves dead to sin but alive for God in Christ Jesus." (Romans 6.3-11).

Our life in this world, even for the most saintly among us, is a mixture of good and evil. We can say that the new Life, which we have freely chosen and entered into through our death and resurrection at Baptism, will be a struggle until the moment we reach the finish line. Christians die as everyone else does, yet we live in the consolation that our physical death is not the end, but a passage into the fullness of life. The real death to sin has occurred before the biological death. "I am the resurrection and the life: whoever believes in me, though he should die, will come to live; and whoever is alive and believes in me, will never die." (John 11.25-26)

The Fullness of Life

What will the fulfillment of life be like? Even in our wildest dreams we cannot imagine it. "Eye has not seen, ear has not heard, nor has it so much as dawned on man what God has prepared for those who love him." (1 Corinthians 2.9) It is an entry into a totally new and previously unexperienced mode of existence. The true self, no longer limited by the bounds of corporality, will be in final and complete union with God. The 'flesh-body' becomes a 'spirit-body.' "This corruptible body must be clothed with incorruptibility, this mortal body with immortality. But when the corruptible frame takes on incorruptibility and the mortal immortality, then will the saying of Scripture be fulfilled: Death is swallowed up in victory. O death, where is your victory? O death, where is your sting?" (1 Corinthians 15.53-55)

Our complex system of sense impressions, nerve impulses, and brain interpretations will come to an end. For the 'spirit-body,' seeing will be intuition, touching will be knowing, hearing will be understanding, tasting will be complete awareness, smelling will be loving. There will be in us an intuitive presence of the whole world, filled with the sweetness and warmth that comes from the earthiness of our senses. Once experienced, this will endure forever.

I suppose heaven could be described in many different ways. John's image of the continual wedding feast appeals strongly to me: the symbol of unending joy and happiness in belonging to the dearest person in our life. It is the joy of perfect and complete mutual giving, the love affair in which I completely lose myself in union with the beloved. I do not really lose myself, but rather I allow my true self to emerge, for perfect union does not destroy, but perfects the parts. It is the unending ecstasy of perfect love.

The world has been slowly and gradually coming through its stages of evolution — cosmogenesis, biogenesis, noogenesis. Our present era could perhaps be described as person-genesis. We are discovering that the fulfillment of human life is becoming truly human. Again we are discovering,

146

through modern psychology, what the Gospel proclaims: the full, mature, human person can only develop by loving and being loved. The world itself will reach its ultimate perfection when true, universal love has penetrated the entire earth. Belief in the Resurrection entails belief that this is possible. With each individual man's entry into eternal life, part of the universe reaches its eternal consummation. Man, in his new life on this earth, anticipates what mankind will become at the consummation of the world.

Reality or Myth?

Perhaps we are sometimes tempted to wonder if the afterlife is only a myth or a dream. Maybe it was the fantasy of the early Christians. It seems so utterly unscientific to believe such a theory that clearly can not be demonstrated.

Reflecting on our analysis of death and what comes after death, we are forced to admit that our basic conclusions have not been demonstrated. Whether we accept or reject the fulfillment of life beyond time and space, ultimately we are forced to say, "I believe." Whether I believe that there is an afterlife or not I cannot prove it. All I can honestly say is, "That's what I believe." This does not make my belief any less true. It is simply unscientific to attempt to demonstrate or prove such conclusions.

What is life without ultimate fulfillment? Have you ever traveled across a long desert road that seems to go nowhere? Life without ultimate fulfillment and consummation would be nonsense, a living hell of senselessness. Sartre and Camus would be right and we Christians the fools.

The Christian bases his life on the reality of the Easter faith which he believes. We are not alone in our quest for the meaning of the afterlife. There is for us the faith of the disciples who witnessed to their Easter experience. The fishermen from Galilee were not gullible and credulous people. They saw the living Lord. The crucified One, who seemed to have been utterly defeated, was experienced as the One who triumphed. After His death He was experienced as living. He approached death with the same freedom and openness to the way of God He had shown throughout His life, and He was able to accept from God, as no other could, the fullness of the Spirit.

It was the Easter experience that gave the first disciples the new life of their faith. They went forth to proclaim the message of new life. This was no passive acceptance of poverty, ignorance, and corruption, but a message that demanded an unequivocal conversion to a completely new life, the creative life of the Spirit. This new life would be victorious, improbable though it may seem, because Jesus had already been victorious. Through faith in the Risen Lord, the disciples entered into a new life, full of dynamic, creative love, in the hope of things to come today, tomorrow, and until the end.

Only one who has hope can see the full reality of faith. Faith with hope experienced and witnessed to by the first followers of Jesus of Nazareth, gives direction and meaning to our lives as Christians today. We see the Church as the fellowship of believers united in the bond of love; through this fellowship we believe in the Risen Lord. Our belief becomes the very ground of our existence. For he who believes, it is impossible to separate belief from life.

Is it intellectually more honest to accept human existence as an absurdity, in which there is no place for hope? It would be if life here were to come to an end and there were no afterlife. The ultimate meaning of man's life cannot be a datum of experience since life's meaning transcends experience. We have the dilemma between absurdity or hope for fulfillment.

In the life of Jesus of Nazareth, the gates of the prison of time have been forced open. We can say: "I believe in the resurrection of the body; I believe in the transformed fulfillment of my whole existence." Our way of the cross has a fifteenth station: time and space release us to enter into the incomprehensible mystery of God's love and life everlasting, a life fully realized only when the world has been transformed, and enters into a state of glory at the end of time.

Appendices

Appendices

chapter notes

Chapter One
None.

Chapter Two

1. Pierre Teilhard de Chardin, *The Phenomenon of Man*, Chapter 11.
2. Ibid., p. 67.
3. Ibid., p. 78.
4. Ibid., p. 87.
5. Ibid., p. 102.
6. Ibid., p. 147.
7. Ibid., p. 148.
8. Ibid. See pp. 152-160, *passim*.
9. Ibid., p. 163.
10. Ibid., pp. 170-171.
11. John Noss, *Man's Religions*, p. 141.

Chapter Three

1. Harvey Cox, *God's Revolution and Man's Responsibility*, pp. 34-39.
2. For a graphic portrayal of sin in the 20th century, see Hannah Arendt, *Eichmann in Jerusalem: A Report on the Banality of Evil.*

Chapter Four

1. "Dogmatic Constitution on Divine Revelation," number 14, *Documents of Vatican II*

Chapter Five

1. Teilhard, *op. cit.*, p. 296.
2. Ibid., pp. 296-297.
3. Ibid., p. 298.
4. Ibid., cf. pp. 260-268.
5. *A New Catechism*, p. 113.

Chapter Six

1. Teilhard, *op. cit.*, p. 265.
2. "Pastoral Constitution on the Church in the Modern World," number 10, *Documents of Vatican II*.
3. Ibid., number 3.
4. "Pastoral Constitution on The Church in The Modern World," number 8.
5. Ibid., number 22.

Chapter Seven

1. See, for example, Jessica Mitford, *The American Way of Death*.
2. Teilhard, "L'Energie spirituelle de la souffrance,"*Oeurves*, Number 7, pp. 256-257. (Author's translation)
3. Teilhard, *The Divine Milieu*, p. 88.

Chapter Eight

1. Teilhard, *The Phenomenon of Man*, p. 81.
2. Ladislaus Boros, *Pain and Providence*, p. 93.
3. Ibid., p. 101.

4. Teilhard, *The Divine Milieu*, p. 83.

5. Ibid., p. 91. See also *Rerum Novarum, Quadrigesimo Anno, Mater et Magistra, Pacem in Terris, Progressio Populorum, Gaudium et Spes.*

Chapter Nine

None.

selected bibliography

Arendt, Hannah. *Eichmann in Jerusalem: A Report on the Banality of Evil.* New York: Viking Press, 1963.

Balthasar, Hans Urs von. *A Theological Anthropology.* New York: Sheed and Ward, 1967.

———— *The Way of the Cross.* New York: Herder and Herder, 1967.

Bastion, Hans Dieter. *Teologia de la Pregunta.* Estella, Spain: Editorial Verbo Divino, 1975.

Boff, Leonard. *Jesucristo Liberador.* Buenos Aires: Libros Latinoamerica, 1976.

Boros, Ladislaus. *The Mystery of Death.* New York: Herder and Herder, 1965.

———— *Pain and Providence.* London: Burns and Oates, 1966.

Buber, Martin. *Between Man and Man.* New York: Macmillan Company, 1967.

Cox, Harvey. *God's Revolution and Man's Responsibility.* Valley Forge: Judson Press, 1965.

Durrwell, Francis X. *The Resurrection.* New York: Sheed and Ward, 1960.

Eliade, Mircea. *From Primitive to Zōn.* New York: Harper and Row, 1967.

Evely, Louis. *Suffering.* New York: Herder and Herder, 1967.

Frankl, Victor. *Man's Search for Meaning*. New York: Washington Square Press, 1967.

Fromm, Eric. *The Art of Loving*. New York: Harper and Row, 1967.

Haag, H. *Is Original Sin in Scripture?* New York: Sheed and Ward, 1969.

Jeremias, Joachim. *The Parables of Jesus*. New York: Scribner's, 1963.

Kaam, Adrian von. *Humanitas: Journal of the Institute of Man* 9, no. 1 (February, 1973).

Küng, Hans. *The Church*. New York: Sheed and Ward, 1967.

———— *The Council in Action: Reflections on the Second Vatican Council*. New York: Sheed and Ward, 1963.

———— *The Council, Reform and Reformation*. New York: Sheed and Ward, 1961.

Lacroix, Jean. *The Meaning of Modern Atheism*. Dublin: Logos Books, 1966.

Laurentin, René. *Liberation, Development and Salvation*. Maryknoll, New York: Orbis Books, 1972.

Lepp, Ignace. *Atheism in Our Time*. New York: Macmillan Company, 1969.

Mateos, Juan. *Beyond Conventional Christianity*. Manila: EAPI Press, 1974.

McGatch, Multon. *Death, Meaning and Morality in Christian Thought and Contemporary Culture*. New York: Seabury Press, 1969.

McKenzie, John. *Myth and Realities*. London: A. Chapman, 1963.

Mooney, Christopher F. *Teilhard de Chardin and the Mystery of Christ*. New York: Harper and Row, 1966.

Mouroux, Jean. *The Meaning of Man*. New York: Doubleday and Co., 1961.

Murphy, Roland and Pierre Benoit, eds. *Immortality and Resurrection*. New York: Herder and Herder, 1970.

Nebreda, Alfonso. *Kerygma in Crisis?* Chicago: Loyola University Press, 1965.

A New Catechism. New York: Herder and Herder, 1967.

Noss, John. *Man's Religions.* New York: Macmillan Company, 1963.

Oraison, Marc. *Death and Then What?* New York: Newman Press, 1969.

Pieper, Joseph. *Death and Immortality.* New York: Herder and Herder, 1969.

Rahner, Karl, S.J. *The Christian Commitment.* New York: Sheed and Ward, 1963.

———— *The Church after the Council.* New York: Herder and Herder, 1969.

———— *The Dynamic Element in the Church. Questiones Disputatae* 12. New York: Herder and Herder, 1964.

Renckens, H. *Israel's Concept of the Beginning.* New York: Herder and Herder, 1964.

Richardson, Alan. *The Miracle Stories of the Gospels.* London: SCM Press, 1964.

Rosa, Peter de. *Christ and Original Sin.* Milwaukee: Bruce and Company, 1967.

Schoonenberg, Piet. *Covenant and Creation.* Notre Dame: University Press, 1967.

Segundo, J. L. *The Community Called Church.* New York: Orbis Books, 1973.

———— *Man and Sin.* Notre Dame: University Press, 1965.

Teilhard de Chardin, Pierre. "L'energie spirituelle de la souffrance," *Oeuvres* 7. Paris: Editions du Seuil, 1963.

———— *The Divine Milieu.* New York: Harper and Row, 1960.

———— *The Phenomenon of Man.* New York: Harper and Row, 1965.

Van Caster, Marcel. "Secularization: A Christian View." *Lumen Vitae* 23 (1968).

Van der Pol, W. J. *The End of Conventional Christianity.* New York: Newman Press, 1968.